Bonnie Martin

Bonnie Martin

My Love Affair with Cuba

Bonnie Martin

BALBOA PRESS
A DIVISION OF HAY HOUSE

Copyright © 2017 Bonnie Martin.

All rights reserved. No part of this book may be used or reproduced by any means, graphic, electronic, or mechanical, including photocopying, recording, taping or by any information storage retrieval system without the written permission of the author except in the case of brief quotations embodied in critical articles and reviews.

Balboa Press books may be ordered through booksellers or by contacting:

Balboa Press
A Division of Hay House
1663 Liberty Drive
Bloomington, IN 47403
www.balboapress.com
1 (877) 407-4847

Because of the dynamic nature of the Internet, any web addresses or links contained in this book may have changed since publication and may no longer be valid. The views expressed in this work are solely those of the author and do not necessarily reflect the views of the publisher, and the publisher hereby disclaims any responsibility for them.

The author of this book does not dispense medical advice or prescribe the use of any technique as a form of treatment for physical, emotional, or medical problems without the advice of a physician, either directly or indirectly. The intent of the author is only to offer information of a general nature to help you in your quest for emotional and spiritual well-being. In the event you use any of the information in this book for yourself, which is your constitutional right, the author and the publisher assume no responsibility for your actions.

Any people depicted in stock imagery provided by Thinkstock are models, and such images are being used for illustrative purposes only.
Certain stock imagery © Thinkstock.

Print information available on the last page.

ISBN: 978-1-5043-7429-3 (sc)
ISBN: 978-1-5043-7430-9 (hc)
ISBN: 978-1-5043-7454-5 (e)

Library of Congress Control Number: 2017901716

Balboa Press rev. date: 03/07/2017

In memory of my mother-in-law Lorraine Martin

"The golden moments in the stream of life rush past
us and we see nothing but sand;
the angels come to visit us, and we only
know them when they are gone."

- George Eliot

Table of Contents

Preface ix

Introduction xi

Section One August 2006 1

Section Two April 2008 19

Section Three April 2009 51

Section Four April 2010 89

Section Five Feb/Mar 2011 131

Section Six April 2012 177

Section Seven April 2013 185

Section Eight May 2014 213

Section Nine July 2015 243

Epilogue - The sum of it all 255

Sources 257

Preface

Life can take many changes when you lose someone you love. For me these changes began after losing my dear mother-in-law, Lorraine, in 2005. To honour her memory, my goal was to try to become somewhat like the woman she was, a loving and giving person.

Newly retired, I wanted to do some travelling, and since my husband doesn't care for travel, my friend Bev said she would be willing to take a trip with me. After checking out a few resorts in different countries, we chose one in Cuba, a place I'd never visited nor knew much about.

Upon arriving, I felt a little intimidated because of things I'd read and heard. The pictures of a stern-looking Fidel Castro that hung all around the airport weren't helping. There was no need for concern. Bev and I spent a wonderful week at a resort in eastern Cuba. Among the things that stood out were the warmth of the Cuban people and their love for their country.

Shortly after I arrived home, the angels changed the course of my life. One day, while I was reading the paper, a small ad from an organization called The View Foundation, a mission that provides assistance to challenged communities, caught my eye. They were recruiting volunteers for Ethiopia, Tanzania and Havana, my interest was piqued. An information session was scheduled in Toronto, so with my daughter, Carene, along for support, we attended the meeting and learned about The View Foundation.

The tentative plan was that the project would take place in the months of July and August, and volunteers could sign up for a minimum of two weeks right up to two months. It didn't take me long to decide this was something I wanted to do, so with the support of my husband, Fred, I signed up for two weeks in August.

Carene and I attended a second meeting in Toronto to go over details. Much to my dismay, I found that the majority of the volunteers were much younger than I. Most were teenagers, and the leaders were in their twenties and early thirties. Concerned that I would feel out of place, Carene gave me a boost of confidence, assuring me everything would work out and that I would fit in with no problem.

In 2006 Cuba was getting ready to celebrate the eightieth birthday of Fidel Castro. Unfortunately, that summer he became quite ill and was hospitalized. The media was rife with rumours that he had died and there were reports that the Cubans in Miami were rejoicing in the streets. I wondered what would happen if he should pass away while The View was in Cuba.

As the date to leave grew closer, I found myself excited about my adventure, yet at the same time quite nervous. About one week before my departure, there was a terrorist plot to blow up ten airplanes travelling from the United Kingdom to the USA and Canada, using liquid explosives. The plot was foiled but, as a result, new security measures were put in place and liquids and gels being carried onto all planes were greatly restricted. This turn of events wasn't helping ease my anxiety, plus, I was receiving daily phone calls from my mother, informing me of the latest updates regarding the situation, asking if I was still going.

Introduction

Let me tell you about a place so near, yet so different from what we in Canada are used to. It is rich in history, some very old, and some recent. The architecture is stunning and reminiscent of a far-away European city. The place I am referring to is the island of Cuba. It's easy to see why, when Christopher Columbus first laid eyes on Cuba he wrote, "Never have human eyes beheld anything so beautiful."

Cuba has some of the most beautiful beaches, along with breathtakingly scenic countryside. The people love to celebrate life. They are friendly, have great respect for their fellow man, love and adore their children, and motherhood is almost sainted. It is the only place I know of where women are truly treated as equals. Life can be a struggle in varying degrees for many, but not unbearable. Some food is difficult to obtain, but no one is starving. Education is paid right through university and health care, one of the best in the world, is free. The arts flourish and the music will make your heart soar.

To be fortunate enough to discover this beautiful country was truly a gift from the angels. I consider Cuba to be a little slice of heaven, but I know not everyone would agree. There is much about Cuba that I don't know, but my feeling is most people there are better off since Fidel Castro came into power on January 1, 1959. He is the longest living dictator, and lovingly referred to as the "Commander-in-Chief".

In 2006 Fidel fell ill, and not long after he turned the reins of power over to his brother Raúl. Raúl has managed to open up the country in some ways, making life a little easier. For example, free enterprise is now allowed and, in 2012 a new law passed allowing people to travel to other countries, but with some limitations. But, as is often the case when changes take place, they don't occur as quickly as some would like.

Section One

August 2006

Bonnie Martin

The View project – 2006

Dan, Melina – 2006

My Love Affair with Cuba

Neighbourhoods

*Habana Vieja (Old Havana) - The historic heart of Havana that is rich in history. Restoration work is an on-going process. The aim is to ensure the revival of both the beauty of Habana Vieja and its original vitality.

*Centro Habana and Prado - A varied quarter, with the *Paseo del Prado*, a tree-lined promenade, (initially built to provide greenery for the citizens,) running through one part.

*Vedado and Plaza - A prestigious residential area for many of the city's leading families. The *Plaza de la Revolución*, or Revolution Square, as well as the Hotel Nacional de Cuba are located there.

Colón - Just off the Paseo del Prado is the barrio where the volunteers from The View resided, in the Hotel Lido.

Lawton (Muraleando) - A barrio on the edge of the city where an artistic community is concentrated.

People You'll Meet

The leaders from The View - Lana, Marjorie and Dan

Our tour guide from Amistad - Lionel

Our bus driver from Amistad - Angel

The artists from Muraleando - Manolo and his wife, Mayra; Martin; Victor; Jesús; Manolete and his wife, Nivia

Chapter One

While in Cuba, The View would stay at the Hotel Lido, a small and basic hotel situated in the barrio of Colón in Centro Habana. It had five floors with a tented dining area on the roof, furnished with plastic tables and chairs, where we would have breakfast and dinner. At the meeting in Toronto, we were told the food would be basic and we might be eating a lot of rice and beans.

It was arranged that we would be working with Amistad, an institute that organizes delegations for international groups visiting Cuba. They would furnish us with a tour guide as well as a bus and driver.

We would work under three leaders, Lana, Marjorie and Dan, and, because most of the volunteers were young, the project had rules. There would be a curfew, and all meals and meetings had to be attended. A meeting would be held every night to discuss the events of the day and learn of up-coming plans. It would end with a round table with everyone relating their high and low point of the day.

We worked Monday to Friday but for the most part had to stay with the group on the week-ends. Different activities would be arranged by the leaders and there were optional excursions offered that we could take at our own expense.

On weekdays we received a wake-up call, met for breakfast, and then boarded the bus that took us to a hospital where we worked cleaning in a section that was under construction. A university student and an older gentleman, Umberto, met us at the hospital to tell us what was to be accomplished that day. Umberto doled out our so-called cleaning tools which consisted of brooms, buckets and rags that were full of holes. We had no soap or cleaning products so cleaning construction dirt with cold water and a rag on the end of a broom proved to be quite challenging.

Each day, I packed my backpack with a large bottle of water, rubber gloves, leather work gloves, and an ever-present and ever-needed sweat rag. A sweat rag is really a face cloth people carry, used to wipe your face when you sweat, and believe me, in Cuba you sweat a great deal. At the end of the shift I turned my rubber gloves inside out to drain the inch or so of sweat that had pooled in the bottom of each finger. My shirt was soaking wet and I was a sweaty, dirty mess.

The amount of attention we received at the hospital proved to be quite amusing. We numbered about fifteen so it was understandable that we garnered some stares. I couldn't figure out why what we were doing was so interesting it would hold people's attention for as long as it did. One day we were working outside in an inner courtyard piling wood to make room for some heavy equipment. I looked up and there were seven people, all in white coats, standing and staring at us. We worked for approximately two hours at the task and they never moved.

The bus picked us up around noon and Lionel brought our lunch that he had picked up from a local restaurant. It was usually spaghetti or sometimes a bun with ham and cheese, and we ate it in our rooms. We had a couple of hours of free time before meeting for our afternoon activity. During the free time, Marjorie offered Spanish lessons in her room, which we were encouraged to attend.

Umberto

Umberto, the older gentleman from the hospital had the kindest face and a gentle demeanour. When he saw me gulping water to ease my thirst, he cautioned me, "Not too much." I later learned that when the normal balance of electrolytes in the body is pushed outside safe limits it can lead to water intoxication. Another day he motioned if he could look at my leather work gloves, which he seemed to like a lot. Assuming he would just like them for working, I made a mental note to give them to him when we were finished the project at the hospital. When I gave them to him, I learned he liked to ride bulls, and that's what he wanted them for.

The volunteers had taken resources to Cuba for all the people we were connected with there. When Dan gave Umberto his small bundle containing some toiletries, razors, T-shirts and shoes, thanking him for helping us, he said Umberto's bottom lip began to quiver and tears trickled down his cheeks. A little goes a long way when people connect.

A Moment in Time – Angel and the garbage men

Garbage is a problem in Havana mainly because of the lack of space to house it. Every street corner has grey bins where people deposit their daily household trash, and, as you might imagine, with the heat, the odour can become quite strong.

One morning while travelling to the hospital we came upon a garbage truck, which was an open-backed dump truck. It was stopped and two garbage men were cleaning up a pile of trash from a bin that had been overturned on the side of the street. Because the streets are so narrow there wasn't room for the bus to pass so we stopped. At first cars stopped behind us; then, realizing this was going to take some time, they began squeezing by. I watched as one garbage man shovelled garbage into a small bin that he tossed to the other man standing in the back of the truck. That man emptied the bin, and then tossed it back to the first man. At the rate they were going I knew we would be there a long time. It did enter my mind that the longer we sat, the less time we would be at the hospital, which was fine with me. After about fifteen minutes Angel, our bus driver, couldn't take it any longer. He got off the bus and approached the garbage men. With arms flailing and a lot of yelling from both sides I was sure a fight would break out. It didn't, but they did move the truck enough so that our bus could get by.

This being the first year The View had visited Cuba, there were unavoidable changes to the plans. By the time I arrived, they had become involved with a group of artists from the barrio of Lawton, also known as Muraleando. The volunteers had travelled to Muraleando on a few occasions to help prepare walls so local artists could adorn them

My Love Affair with Cuba

with murals. Without these murals, the walls would be faded, peeling and drab.

Because some of the original plans had not worked out, the leaders came up with a new one. Volunteers, along with some artists from Muraleando, would work with children from the barrio of Colón on a photography project. I had carried thirty-five disposable cameras to Cuba with me. We held an initial meeting with the artists, the volunteers, and the children on the Paseo del Prado to get the project underway. With Marjorie translating, we sat in a circle and introduced ourselves. Lana explained what the project would entail and then we taught the children a little about photography. Over the next few days we all ventured out to various locations, taking a few pictures every day. Each day had a theme, and the pictures were to relate to the day's theme.

During the meeting I noticed we were being watched. A *policía*, with a very large German shepherd dog, stood near us and while nothing was said, the *policía* never took his eyes off us. I later learned from Lana that The View was being watched on a regular basis.

The whole experience involving the children was an absolute thrill for them. I'm sure most of them had never ridden in a bus as nice as ours, and on some of our outings they were treated to a can of soda. One day we were stopped on the *Malecón* enjoying our drinks when we decided that our group should have a name. Everyone was giving suggestions, when one of the young girls, Melina, came up with the winner. We would call ourselves Friends Forever, a name which turned out to be very fitting.

*The Malecón is a seafront promenade that winds alongside the city's historic quarters from the Colonial centre to the skyscrapers of Vedado. It is a meeting place for young and old alike. People sit on the wall that runs the entire length, enjoying each other's company, sometimes sharing a bottle of rum.

Friends Forever was going to the beach! Our leaders stressed that we would have to be very responsible and watch our charges carefully.

In Cuba, drivers take great pride in their buses, and our driver, Angel, wasn't fussed on having his full of people with beach sand all over them, so there were rules for the bus. We were to make sure that before we re-boarded we had brushed the sand off us and our clothes.

After lunch we all met outside the hotel, boarded the bus and set off to a beach used mainly by the locals. It was beautiful with white soft sand and turquoise water glistening in the sun.

Cuban beachgoers are very different from what I'm used to. I live in a town situated on the shore of Lake Huron, so in the summer, tourists and locals alike love to go to the beach. They arrive with paraphernalia ranging from blankets, towels, chairs, beach umbrellas, floats, toys, balls, and coolers full of food and drink. In Cuba people arrive with almost nothing other than what they are wearing. You might see the odd umbrella but there are almost no towels and very few toys. I watched some children playing with an empty rum bottle that they filled with water and then poured over each other's heads. The game went on for a long time, keeping them greatly amused.

When I go to the beach I usually sit and read, then take a dip to cool off, but this wasn't going to be that kind of beach day for me. I heard my name being called and realized some of the artists wanted me to join them in the water for a game of catch with a tiny football. We threw the ball to each other until I thought my arms would fall off. Later, we all lazed on the beach, played with the children in the water, took some photos and had a fun-filled afternoon.

Before returning to the bus, we made sure we had brushed the sand off. But at the bus, there was Angel with a pail of water and he had a plan. He would pour a little over our feet and legs then we would dry them before we boarded.

My Love Affair with Cuba

A Moment in Time – One Planet, One People......
Please

A dance troupe from California, associated with the Baha'i faith, arrived at the Hotel Lido one day. Our group became acquainted with them so we invited them to join us for salsa lessons planned that night in the dining area of the hotel.

Irasema, a dancer from Lawton, had come to the hotel a couple of nights before to teach us how to dance salsa and it had been great fun. This particular night was Irasema's birthday so Dan bought a cake and we planned to turn our salsa lesson into a party with our new amigos.

We all danced and danced then the troupe said they wanted to perform for us. They explained the number they would perform depicted African roots. They stood in three rows, four abreast, and no words were spoken, just clapping, slapping their thighs and stomping to tell the story. It was all very moving, bringing Irasema to tears. She told them they had touched her deep in her soul. Another girl from the troupe recited a poem she had written about growing up in Los Angles among gangs, and one of our volunteers, an aspiring poet recited a poem she had written.

Following is an entry from my journal, written when I went back to my room that night:

> It is twelve-thirty a.m. and I have only experienced such a high a few times in my life. This one is right up there with giving birth. This whole experience just keeps getting better and better. I can't believe I was feeling uneasy about doing this.

Irasema and a few of us were going to visit Hammel's Alley, a working class quarter with deep Afro roots, to attend a rumba festival.

*Rumba is the African soul of Cuban music, originating in poor neighbourhoods as a voice of rebellion against slavery and segregation.

It then became a form of political satire and social criticism, as well as the poignant expression of an unhappy love affair.

When we arrived at Hammel's Alley a light rain was falling and there didn't seem to be anything happening. After some confusion we all ended up at the door of a Santería priest who informed us there had been a death in the community so there would be no dancing today. Because it was raining, she invited us into her humble home. She was dressed completely in white, which is how aspiring priests must dress for an entire year. There was an altar in one corner of the room and plaques on the wall depicting the different Orishas, which are gods in the Santería religion. Ian, one of the volunteers, and a devout Catholic, asked if he might say some prayers at her altar. Permission was granted and then she began to explain a little about Santería to us.

*Santería is a religion that exists in Cuba as the result of its history. Slaves from Nigeria merged their gods' identities with certain Catholic saints, and over the years the two religions have almost become blended. Santería is so strongly felt that it is an important part of the national identity.

As the priest explained things, I found myself becoming emotional. She noticed, and beckoned me, along with Irasema, into another room to perform a type of cleansing ritual for me.

A Moment in Time – Experiencing Santería

The priest took a glass and half filled it with water, then dropped a small wooden cross into it. I was told to cup my hands so that she could squirt a small amount of a pink, pleasant smelling liquid into them. Irasema motioned for me to throw this liquid on me; my arms, legs and face, then throw it off and snap my fingers toward the vessel with the cross.

After I did that the priest took what looked like a lump of fine pink coloured sand and rubbed it on the back of my neck, my arms and my legs. I then repeated the throwing it off and snapping of my fingers. She explained someone (an ancestor maybe) from long ago cried a lot and that's why I do. This ritual would help to stop it. She told Irasema to bring me back Sunday at two o'clock for a more extensive ritual. After we left, Irasema told me that some Santería priests can be schemers and might try and take advantage of me by telling me they would fix my problems for a fee. Irasema said she would perform a ritual on me the next day, out of love.

On Sunday, Irasema arrived just after lunch, and with Chantel along to translate, we headed to my room to begin the ritual. Irasema had brought an egg and some shells, and I had purchased a candle the day before, on her instruction. She lit the candle and told me to fill a glass with water. I was to ask a question after which she would shake the shells and drop them. The way they landed told her the answer. I became very emotional and Irasema instructed me on what I should do to handle what was troubling me. Every so often she would sprinkle some of the water from the glass on me, and told me I was to leave the glass of water under my bed and it would help ease my sadness. When the ritual was over the three of us went up to the roof where Irasema took the egg and threw it over her shoulder. She instructed me to not look where the egg had landed. When it was all over I felt totally drained but I did feel good.

We wanted to hold a photo exposition and host a party for everyone that had been involved in the project. To get ready for the exposition, we travelled to Muraleando with the children to meet with the artists and choose our favourite pictures, which we then co-ordinated and framed.

Manolo helped find the perfect location in Vedado to hold both events. The exposition would be held in a beautiful old mansion, now used for music and dance lessons, and the party would take place in a banquet facility directly across the road.

With the children's remaining photos, we would help them make individual albums that they could decorate, so they would have a memento of the project. Since we needed a spot to work with construction paper and glue, a family with two children in the project volunteered their home, which was on the roof of a tenement, so they had the perfect set-up for us to spread out and work.

A Moment in Time – Being busted in Cuba

Everyone was busy working when two policemen appeared on the outdoor part of the roof. The lady of the house and our three leaders approached them and they all stood talking. Dan told us to take the resources, go back to our rooms and stay there until we heard from them. Needless to say, everyone was very nervous and worried that the family would be in trouble for allowing us into their home.

The policemen escorted the leaders to the hotel to check our passports, which were locked in the hotel safe. They began asking questions about what we were doing in Cuba and it seemed they were trying to intimidate. They would ask a question but not give Marjorie a chance to answer before asking another one. They stated our tourist visas were the wrong ones, and since we were on a project, we needed working visas. They insisted we either get the proper visas or we would be deported. When Marjorie explained we were leaving in two days they relented somewhat. In the end the policemen shook hands with the leaders and wished them well. It turned out they were only doing their jobs and really had no ill will against us.

We all met in Lana's room for a meeting and emotions were running high. Personally, I was furious that this had occurred, feeling that The View should have had everything worked out before we went to Cuba. We were told we would learn more at our meeting that night.

The leaders met with our tour guide Lionel, as well as the Committees for the Defense of the Revolution, (CDR), representative. Lionel got in touch with the authorities and was told we had to cease our involvement with the children. When he explained we were planning on hosting a party for them, he was told they couldn't attend. At that point the CDR became involved saying she would get permission, which was granted, but we could have nothing to do with getting them there. They weren't allowed on our bus nor could we pay for taxis to take them. The CDR said she would make sure the children got to the party somehow.

At our meeting that night we learned some of what had gone on, but we still didn't know if the children would make the party or not. Everyone discussed the matter and we decided, for the sake of the artists and other people invited, we should go through with our plans.

*CDR – Committees for the Defense of the Revolution

CDRs are a network of neighbourhood committees across Cuba. There are CDRs on every block and it is their duty to monitor the activities of each person on their respective blocks. An individual file is kept on each block resident, some of which reveal the internal dynamics of households.

This all sounds very oppressive, but defenders note that CDRs have other important responsibilities that include arranging festivals, administering many voluntary community projects, and other things to help the Cuban people. Our experience with the CDR in Colón was a positive one because she did all she could to help the situation.

A Moment in Time – A party to remember

On the day of our party, we all hoped for the best. The morning was spent putting the children's albums together, but we left the decorating to them.

We donned our finest attire then Lionel and the bus picked us up after lunch. We waited outside the mansion for the artists, and, we hoped, the children, to arrive. When the artists arrived, we went inside to view the photos, now framed and hung gallery style in two large rooms.

With still no sign of the children, we reluctantly headed across the street for the party. There was food and soft drinks for everyone and we made sure to save some should the children arrive. After we finished eating, a couple of volunteers went outside to watch for them and a little later they came back excitedly announcing, "The children are here!" Dan remarked through tears, "Now it's a party."

As the children and their parents entered the venue, what stood out to me was their appearance. I had become used to seeing most of them dressed simply in a pair of shorts for the boys and shorts and a T-shirt for the girls, usually with bare feet. Today everyone was in their best finery, wearing crisp outfits and shoes with snowy white socks.

As they enjoyed the food we had saved for them, something happened I'll never forget. Victor, one of the artists who had shown a lot of interest in the project, arrived, sweating profusely. We learned he had walked for two hours to attend.

The party was a huge success with lots of dancing and socializing and once again, I found myself on another emotional high.

Although I didn't realize it at the time, the angels had been at work for me. While we had been looking at our photos, Jesús, one of the artists, approached me to chat. He asked about my life and then gave me his business card that stated he was a tourist guide. I tucked the card away and thought no more about it.

Tonight would be our last dinner at the Hotel Lido and, when we headed up for the meal, a wonderful surprise awaited us. The kitchen staff had gone out of their way to make our last dinner a special one, taking the regular food supplied, and with loving care, turned it into a beautifully displayed buffet feast. As they all stood beaming beside their creation, we all walked up and thanked them. They told us they loved having us at the hotel and voiced how concerned they were when they thought we were in trouble with the authorities.

After dinner we had a short meeting to relay our highs and lows of the day. Most highs were that the children had made it to the party. When it was Ian's turn to speak, he said his high was that the leaders had managed to pull it all off. He completely broke down and was unable to continue. It was all pretty intense and clear that this experience meant a lot to us.

Chapter Two

Our last day mainly entailed taking care of last-minute chores. We were granted some free time so we split up and everyone went about their business. I spent a lovely afternoon with two volunteers and Victor, one of the artists, walking around Old Havana. Because Victor knew a lot of artists there, he took us to visit some of their small galleries. We all did our own thing for dinner, and later walked to the Malecón with some of the children to say our good-byes.

We had put all the gifts we had brought for the children together, but we had to find a way to get them to them without the authorities knowing. We put everything into large hockey bags which Dan gave to a friend from the neighbourhood who would discreetly give them to the children.

The bus arrived at four in the morning to take us to the airport. When I came outside, there sitting on the sidewalk were some of the older boys from the barrio and a few parents waiting to say good-bye. It seemed we were going to be missed. The View had spent two months with these people bringing some new experiences and joy into their lives. They in turn had repaid us with their openness and friendship.

Observations and Reflections - 2006

My experience in Cuba with The View was life-changing. I experienced so many "Moments in Time" that it's hard to believe they all occurred in two short weeks. I knew I had to return and find out more about this wonderful country that is misunderstood by so many.

Because the Hotel Lido is very small, we got to know many of the staff. As our project was nearing the end, they began dropping hints for things they wanted us to give them. I understood it must have been difficult for them to see us with so much when they have so little. It was a lesson in human nature.

Cubans love it when it rains. It is nature's way of cleaning the streets and refreshing the air.

Section Two

April 2008

Yosiet's studio, Muraleando – 2008

Dinner at the Lazaro's - 2008

People You'll Meet

The Lazaros

This is the family who allowed The View to use their home to make our photo albums with the children. I have only now learned some of their names so I refer to them as "The Lazaros". The family consists of the father, the mother, Mariela, Lazaro and Melina, who participated in the project with The View, and Kmilo, the youngest brother. The oldest son Yonmay lives one floor below with Mariela's mother.

Jesús Magan - Tour Guide, Artist

Jesús proved to be invaluable to us. He generally makes our time in Cuba very enjoyable by making arrangements and, while showing us around, translates. He is married to Maria and they have a daughter, Jenny.

Juan Antonio - Tour Guide, Photographer

Juan Antonio is the brother-in-law of Jesús and he and Jesús work together as tour guides and photographers. Over the years we have hired Juan many times, especially when travelling outside Havana. He is married to Mari and has a grown son.

Manuel M. Díaz Baldrich (Manolo) - Coordinador General of Muraleando, Artist

It was Manolo's vision that started the community project that came to be known as Muraleando in 2001. He lives with his wife Mayra, who is his, and Muraleando's, greatest supporter, and they have a daughter and son. Their house is a gathering place for members and friends of Muraleando.

Nivia Herrera Lopez - Artist
Manuel Díaz Rosario (Manolete) - Print Maker

Nivia is one of the few female artists in Muraleando and her husband Manolete is a print maker.

Victor Francisco Hernandez Mora, (the tall one) - Artist

Victor is one of the most dedicated artists in Muraleando. He is well over six feet and is quick to laugh. In 2006 when I asked Victor what he would do if he wasn't an artist, his response was, "If I couldn't be an artist, I wouldn't want to live."

Miguel Martin Ortiz (Martin) - Artist

Martin is second-in-command in Muraleando and is sometimes jokingly referred to as El Commandante. He and Manolo have been friends for many years.

Mario Delgado Sotomayor or MC Mario (his professional name)

Mario is a Spanish rap artist and very good at what he does. He speaks English and continues to take classes to improve his language skills. He has overcome many obstacles in his life. When he moved in with his sister-in-law in Muraleando, he was welcomed by the community. He scraped walls, built scaffolds, and took on whatever the task at hand might be. He says without Muraleando, he would just be sitting on some street corner.

Victor Rodriguez - (the older one)

I first met Victor (the older one) in 2009. He is an old friend of Jesús from their days together in Russia and speaks English. He is a public relations person for Muraleando leading tours for people from English-speaking countries when they visit. He also translates videos and documentaries about Muraleando into English.

Yosiet Quintero Urra - Ceramic and Raku artist

Yosiet is a gentle man whose feelings run deep. He lives with his wife, son and daughter in the back of his studio.

Tony and Erminda

Tony and Erminda are Manolo's in-laws and live on the ground floor of the house where Manolo and his family live. Erminda helps Mayra with cooking for guests and events in Muraleando. Tony acts as a driver when needed and sees to other Muraleando chores.

Irasema   Instructor of Dance

Irasema is a dance teacher contributing to Muraleando that way. I make a point of seeing her at least once when I visit Muraleando.

Chapter Three

It had been close to two years since I had visited Cuba, but I still thought about my experiences there often. The country and the people impacted me greatly and I felt it pulling me back. I asked my daughter, Carene, if she would be interested in accompanying me on a trip there and she said she would love to.

We arrived in Havana in all our glory and breezed into the breathtakingly beautiful Hotel Nacional de Cuba. The name sounds as regal as the hotel looks, and rolls off your tongue with purpose even if, like us, you barely speak Spanish.

Back in the day, before the Revolution, the Hotel Nacional de Cuba was where many celebrities and other important people stayed. Outside some of the rooms are pictures of stars depicting that the room was their favourite.

After checking in, we did a quick change then headed out to explore the hotel's grounds, marvelling at the beauty before us. What is referred to as The Veranda, runs along three sides of the hotel and has big wicker chairs, couches and tables, with a bar tucked into one corner. There were people sitting and relaxing, sipping cocktails or café while chatting. We wandered a little farther to the edge of the huge rock the hotel sits upon, overlooking the water. We took a seat at a table and ordered the first of the many mojitos we would drink while in Cuba. It was now around two o'clock and with the sun glistening on the water, the Malecón below, and a view of the city, we smiled at each other and remarked how lucky we were to be there. It was magnificent!

After an early dinner we thought we would go for a walk on the Malecón and see where we ended up. As we got closer to Old Havana, I thought I'd try to see if I could find the Hotel Lido, where I had stayed in 2006. After many twists and turns we were there. We stood looking at the hotel and memories came flooding back. When I felt someone tugging at my sleeve, I turned around and realized it was Angel, one of the young boys from the barrio. He beamed at us and I'm sure he was wondering what I was doing there. I asked, "Lazaro?" He nodded and as he began leading us in the direction of Lazaro's home, I saw a group of people on the street listening to someone speaking. Amongst them were Lazaro's mother, Mariela, and his sister, Melina. I approached Mariela and she was very surprised to see me. She greeted us warmly then left the meeting and invited us to her home. I later learned the person speaking was a medical representative telling the neighbourhood people there was dengue fever about and what precautions to take. Some might think that would take precedence over two Canadians showing up unannounced, but this was Cuba.

We followed Mariela, leaving Angel looking very pleased with himself, and went up one floor to her mother's apartment. Even though I had never met her, she also greeted us warmly and told us to sit down. Mariela went to find Lazaro and before long reappeared with him. He was now seventeen and still the sweet young man I remembered. Communication was difficult but we managed, and did figure out we were being asked to come for café the following day at two o'clock. When we were leaving, I could see that Angel had been busy rounding up some neighbourhood children. Sitting outside the apartment door were about five children who shyly greeted me. Walking back to the hotel I was so giddy I could hardly contain myself.

One of the things I'd hoped to accomplish on this trip was to get in touch with Jesús Magan. He had given me his business card in 2006 that told me he was a tour guide, so I wanted to hire him to make our trip more enjoyable. When I tried to reach him by telephone our first morning, the woman who answered told me in halting English that Jesús would be home the next day so I said I would call him then.

Because it was a Saturday, I knew there would be a lot going on in Old Havana, so we headed that way. People were out and about doing their daily business. Many were lining up to buy food for the day. Not everyone has refrigeration, and during the Special Period black-outs were common, so people got used to shopping daily. There seemed to be men repairing things everywhere. Because so much is difficult to obtain in Cuba, people repair things until they just can't be repaired any longer. There were bands playing, and women with Churchill cigars that they would pop into their mouths when a tourist walked by and pose for a picture. Their aim was to be paid a few pesos.

The Special Period

The Special Period is the name given to the time after the Soviet Union dissolved. It resulted in the abrupt withdrawal of economic subsidies, making gasoline, transport, food, and material goods in short supply. The Cuban people were asked to endure shortages for the sake of the survival of the socialist revolution. It began in 1989 and declined in severity towards the end of the nineties. It was a very difficult time for Cuba.

We had to cut our time short because we had our café date with the Lazaros. No vehicles are allowed in the inner city, so we walked out and hailed a *cocotaxi* to take us back to the hotel. Cocotaxis are fun little egg-shaped scooters exclusively for tourists that can carry two passengers as well as the driver. They are especially fun when they drive on the Malecón and the sea spray comes over the wall and splashes the riders.

Because Havana sits beside the sea, the salt air, along with the sun, has taken a toll on some of the buildings. There is a program in effect to re-build in keeping with the original architecture wherever possible. It is too late for some of the buildings, which have literally fallen down but, with a little imagination you can envision how beautiful the city was in days gone by.

Over the years, and several visits, I have had the privilege of being inside quite a few of the older buildings. In some of what are now very humble dwellings, there is an abundance of marble and beautiful hanging light fixtures from the past.

When we arrived at Lazaro's we found him and his sister Melina waiting for us outside. We made our way up to their home and I was pleased to discover they now had a permanent walkway leading to it. When I had first visited with The View, we had to cross from one side of the building to the other by walking on loosely laid planks, while trying not to look down at the empty space twenty feet below. The whole experience had scared me to death. I had brought a few small gifts for the family as well as some photos taken in 2006 of children from the barrio with volunteers from The View. We were served café, the Cuban way, in white demitasse cups, pre-sweetened, black and delicious. Even with the language barrier, we had a very nice visit and, with the help of a calendar, realized we were being invited to dinner on Wednesday evening. I wondered how we would communicate during the evening, but I certainly wasn't going to decline. We said our good-byes until Wednesday then headed back to the hotel. As we sat on The Veranda and talked about our day over mojitos, my heart was full.

The next morning I was successful reaching Jesús. It didn't take him long to place me and, when I explained the situation, saying we wanted to hire him, he was keen and suggested we meet him in the lobby of the hotel in about an hour.

After greetings and introductions, we sat and visited for a few minutes, catching up on our news. He told us we had picked a great time to visit because in April, Muraleando celebrates their birthday and there are always events taking place. He said two artists, a mother and daughter, were visiting from Toronto, working on a special project. There was a concert planned for Wednesday evening and he would arrange everything for us to attend. When I reflected on our perfect timing, I knew the angels had been at work.

Jesús asked me what I wanted to do today so I said I would like to walk around Vedado, which is where the Hotel Nacional is located. It is a beautiful section of Havana, with many old mansions, some of which have been turned into embassies. There is an abundance of lush greenery, giving it a peaceful, quiet feeling.

After Jesús made sure we had water and hats we struck off. He pointed out restaurants and small jazz clubs that he thought we would enjoy in the evenings. Walking past people in a long line-up, he explained it was the queue for the Coppelia ice cream parlour, and that people will wait for over an hour for ice cream. He excitedly pointed out Havana's new city buses. I had seen the old *camel buses* in 2006 so I knew why the new ones thrilled him. Camel buses, a Havana invention from the Special Period, were a tractor that pulled a long trailer with humps shaped like a camel. They were designed to carry as many people as possible and could hold up to three hundred. With no ventilation and usually crowded, people had to use caution, holding their purses and wallets close, as pickpockets would rob people on a regular basis. Women also had a problem with constantly being groped, so there were buses that were for women only. One day in 2006 I had witnessed people trying to board a camel bus and it was a sight to behold. They pried open the back doors and entered that way, literally heaving small children in through an open back window.

 We hadn't ventured very far when Jesús met a woman he knew. They greeted each other the Cuban way which entails embracing and a kiss on one cheek. We were introduced to Consuelo de la Angelos, once an architect, now an artist. It was explained that Consuelo lived in a wooden house which is a rarity in Cuba, made from wood imported from New Orleans. Jesús said that we should visit. Things were moving a little quickly for me as I wasn't used to Jesús' way of stating things in a very matter-of-fact way, but I was eager to catch up.

 We walked along with Jesús pointing out buildings and embassies and before long another friend came along. He was a man in his late sixties, wearing a funky sun hat, with his arm in a cast. We were introduced and told he was from Paris but spends a great deal of time in Cuba. He had been in Algiers when he fell and broke his arm so he decided to heal in Cuba. He and Jesús knew each other from translating work in past years. I asked him how many languages he spoke and was told four, and struggles with a couple more. I wondered if these friends of Jesús could get any more interesting.

 Jesús told us he was taking us to a rumba festival in Hammel's Alley so he hailed a taxi. April is the month of festivals in Cuba so we really had chosen well.

Callejón de Hammel, or Hammel's Alley is a working-class barrio that, on Saturdays, becomes a venue for rumba shows. I soon realized this was where I had been with The View when I had been introduced to Santería. Today there was a top-rated band performing, along with singers and dancers. A little girl of about five danced with the group, learning the dance while she participated. It was very hot and crowded, with little air, so I'm afraid we didn't last long.

It was time for lunch so Jesús tried to hail a taxi. Taxis are scarce in the poorer areas, but he did manage to flag down one of the old cars, a 1955 Chevrolet that had seen better days. The old cars that are used for taxis aren't supposed to take tourists, but Jesús sweet-talked the driver who said he would take us, but drop us off on one of the back streets close to our destination which turned out to be Centro Habana and Prado, the area where I had stayed in 2006.

Jesús turned into a doorway and proceeded up some stairs to a *paladar*. *Paladares* are small private restaurants, usually in a section of someone's home, and are licensed by the state. At that time each paladar could have no more than twelve seats but in 2010 the law was changed to allow up to twenty. They are a good option when eating out in Cuba, with dishes that are often simple but usually good.

We were seated on a balcony overlooking the Paseo del Prado and memories came back of the times I had spent sitting on the tree-lined boulevard taking in the sights and sounds. Our meal was outstanding but with far too much food. I was in a dilemma because I knew we would never be able to finish it. I had learned in 2006 that wasting food wasn't done in Cuba. I noticed Jesús push some of his pork aside and then ask the waitress something. She returned with a small box for his leftovers and he said he would be happy to take ours also. I felt a lot better and he was pleased to have meat for the family meal that night.

When we continued walking, we couldn't help but notice the streets were not only quiet, they seemed to be almost deserted. Jesús remembered there was a very important baseball game on TV, a final, and Cubans love baseball.

Since we were close to the Lazaros, we walked over to try to rearrange our dinner date. We were supposed to go on Wednesday evening, but that was the scheduled night of the concert in Muraleando. When we approached Lazaro's doorway, there were two neighbourhood women sitting and chatting so we inquired after Lazaro. They directed us to go upstairs but, when we reached Gramma's door, it seemed there was no one home. Just as one of the ladies came up to check on us, we heard a man from inside calling, telling us to wait. He came down from somewhere above, apologizing for keeping us waiting, saying he was watching the baseball game. Jesús explained our problem to him and, after they exchanged phone numbers, he told me it would all be worked out. He was given an up-date on the game, and as he made our apologies for the interruption, the man told him, "No problem, your friends are my friends."

When I voiced my concerns about being able to communicate with the Lazaros at dinner, Jesús, again in his matter-of-fact way, told me, "Don't worry, I will arrange for my brother-in-law Juan Antonio to meet you there and translate." I wondered how the Lazaros would feel about an uninvited dinner guest, but I put my faith in Jesús. I realized how much easier this trip was going to be with his help.

We continued our tour, learning about Cuba as Jesús translated what was written on the many plaques outside the old buildings. In The Hotel Sevilla we looked at pictures hanging on the walls that included many gangsters, most taken in the fifties. We walked farther and came upon a street that they close once a month for a fruit and vegetable market. It was now around three o'clock so some of the vendors had left but the street was still lively. We were offered tastes of things unfamiliar to us while Jesús looked for mangos for his daughter, Jenny, saying that she loved them. Earlier he had bought her a movie, and it was easy to see just how much he doted on his little girl.

Next we came to Barrio Chino, the Chinese quarter in Havana. There was a large gate at the entrance with a pagoda roof, but other than that, the buildings were much the same as in other areas. Through the gate the area was packed with people standing at the entrances of the many restaurants holding up their menus to coax customers in.

*Barrio Chino

The first Chinese arrived in Cuba in the mid-1800s to work in the sugar industry, and they were treated like slaves. Some of the first to gain their freedom began cultivating small plots of land in Havana. It was in one of those plots that Cuba's first mangos were grown. The second wave of Chinese immigrants arrived from California in the late 1800s with their American savings and started to open restaurants. Members of the Chinese community also fought for Cuban independence.

While we were walking along, Jesús saw a young woman with a friend, and he stopped to talk with her. We learned that the woman was the niece of his first wife and at one time they had all lived together. He said he remembered the woman's mother being out in the streets looking for milk for the child during the Special Period. At that time his wife was very unhappy and wanted to leave Cuba. Jesús was travelling a great deal with his government translating job and times were difficult. Finally, they split and she went to live in Florida. When I asked if they had children together he told me no, he thought it would have been obscene to have a child during that time. He said people were almost starving and artists were unable to paint as their eyesight was failing because of lack of vitamins.

When Jesús turned into yet another doorway and began to climb the stairs, we followed and learned we were now at his house. He lived with his wife Maria, and their daughter, Jenny, as well as two nephews of Maria's who were staying with them for a year. Their dachshund puppy promptly assumed the position for a belly scratch and, when Carene obliged, she was rewarded with small nips from his razor-sharp baby teeth. Dachshunds are a popular breed in Cuba because they are small and also gentle. This one was too cute for words. On a small balcony there was a cardboard box, a bowl of water and a food dish containing a slice of tomato. Meat is scarce in Cuba so pets don't get a lot. We were given a tour of the apartment with Jesús proudly showing us the newly installed ceramic tile in the kitchen. It was only a small section but to them it was like a complete kitchen renovation. The apartment was large with high ceilings and two bathrooms which is rare in Cuba. He told us they were very happy living there. We made our plans for the next day, and when I asked what I owed him, he shyly told me he usually charges 25 Cuban Convertible pesos (CUC), but felt he should give us a deal. I gladly gave him 30 CUC.

CUC – Cuban Convertible pesos

The Cuban Convertible peso is the currency used by tourists in Cuba and is roughly equivalent to the US dollar.

Back at the hotel we freshened up then went to The Veranda for mojitos. We talked about how wonderful the day had been saying it was karma that had made this all come about.

That night we thought we would check out one of the restaurants Jesús had recommended and maybe take in some jazz. We chose La Roca and, when we entered, we could tell it was a happening place. Apparently, Cubans like to dine out on Sundays. While we were trying to decipher the Spanish menu, a young waitress approached to ask if we needed some help. We told her yes, and after a few questions decided on pork and of course mojitos to start. From where I was sitting I could see the area where the servers congregated. They were mainly young people, with an older woman supervising, and it was plain to see that this establishment was run very professionally. All the servers were dressed smartly in navy pants and vests with a white shirt. When one of the waiters had trouble communicating with us he excused himself and went to the supervisor for help. Instead of her coming to the table, she told him what to say and after thinking for a moment he returned and was successful. While we sat enjoying a delicious meal we took in our surroundings. Beside us, a table with three ladies and a gentleman were laughing and having a good time then quietly began to sing. They ended up with the man and one of the ladies doing what seemed to be a love song. When they finished, Carene and I clapped, and they smiled at us.

When the bill arrived I was shocked to see the grand total was 9 CUC. Thank you, Jesús! It had been a full day so we decided to forgo the jazz. While we were walking back to the hotel, gazing at the full moon, a young man began walking beside us and commented on *La Luna*. He then motioned that I should have my purse over my shoulder, not just in my hand. I wondered who he was warning us about because so far everyone here had been so nice. Back in our room as I sat writing in my journal while Carene slept peacefully, I was feeling very mellow, sentimentally deep and just high on life.

On one of the outer fringes of Havana lies the barrio of Lawton. As is the case in most barrios in Havana, the people struggle, but Cubans seem to live by a rule of helping their fellow man any way they can.

Lawton happens to have a concentration of artists, and one, a man named Manolo, heads a community project. In 2001 he had a vision and formed a group with some other artists who work very hard to make the community a better place to live. Manolo invented the name *Muraleando* (literally "muraling" or mural-making). Since then, the barrio is informally called Muralcando by many.

The artists of Muraleando paint murals on paint-starved walls around the barrio, as well as build small monuments. They hold workshops for children where they can paint and do different craft projects. When in Muraleando, it seems like you are in a land of make believe. Lovely murals, many telling a story, are painted on the outside walls of homes. At the bus stop there was no seat, so the artists made one by welding old car wheels together, painting them in bright colours and then topped them with a stone slab.

Through the years Muraleando has grown, attracting visitors and contributors from many countries. The project provides artists, residents, and children the space and opportunity to express themselves, transforming the barrio into a peoples' art gallery.

Manolo, who holds the title Coordinador General of Muraleando is a tall man, who, not long after meeting, you can't help but like. He lives on the upper floor of a house with his wife, Mayra, and their daughter and son. Mayra's parents live on the ground floor with more family. Their house is a hive of activity with people always coming and going. On the roof is a studio where the artists store their work and some workshops are held.

When the project was a mere two years old, Manolo was asked what the greatest accomplishments of the project have been. He replied that the project has managed to physically transform our community, converting it into a People's Art Gallery. The changes are spiritual as well as physical. A sense of belonging has developed in the barrio where people get involved and concern themselves more and more with solving problems with our own efforts.

Jesús had been hard at work for us. We were visiting Muraleando and, while we drove there in a taxi, he informed us of the day's plan. We would visit the studio of a ceramic artist, new to Muraleando, where we could make a clay tile, paint a ceramic one or do both. Lunch had been arranged for us at Manolo's where we would meet the two artists visiting from Toronto as well as see the artists I had worked with in 2006. It was shaping up to be a wonderful day and I was very excited.

As we drove through the city, Jesús explained the history of the barrios we were passing through and pointed out the power plant that burned diesel. Between the black smoke spewing from it, and the old cars burning who-knows-what, the air quality in Havana isn't the best.

We pulled up to what looked like a large garage and a young, handsome man greeted us. Jesús introduced us to Yosiet who, he said, was the best ceramic artist in Muraleando. Yosiet laughingly replied that he was the only ceramic artist in Muraleando. We entered the building that contained a couple of old cars on one side and, on the other, a studio with some pieces of ceramic work on display. Behind, was a workshop with a kiln made by Yosiet. There was shelving holding ceramic pieces in various stages of completion, as well as manuals. Work surfaces consisted of a couple of tables with some chairs, all made from recycled materials. On the wall was a picture of Yosiet sitting in the lotus position, floating above a cloud. Once, the front of the building had housed pigs, but everything had been scoured clean and it was now as neat as a pin. We were introduced to Yosiet's wife, who was sipping green tea with Lynn, one of the artists from Toronto. Lynn was also there to make a clay tile while her daughter, Real, worked with the other artists. We were offered café which we accepted. A small, stern-looking cat wandered around keeping watch and Yosiet relayed she was a bad-tempered cat. When I laid my canvas purse down on the floor she promptly curled up and went to sleep. The biggest roach I've ever seen waddled by and was completely ignored by the cat. It seemed the roach and the cat had learned to co-habit nicely.

Jesús was going to leave for a couple of hours to work with Real and the other artists on the special project for 2008, which would be a map of the barrio done in glass blocks. Real had brought a tool from Canada used in glass work and had donated it to Muraleando.

As Yosiet prepared the clay for our tiles, we sipped our café and visited with Lynn while she translated for us. I told her I was really no artist and relayed a story I had recently been reminded of. In a Grade Ten art class we were to draw a character from the book *Great Expectations* and I chose Miss Havisham. When the teacher came to have a look, as hard as she tried, she just couldn't hold back her laughter. She told me, "I'm sorry Bonnie, but your Miss Havisham looks like a French Poodle." Lynn assured me not to worry, just have fun. I kept telling myself, "Think abstract, Bonnie, think abstract."

Yosiet gave us a piece of paper and a pencil, suggesting we draw what we might put on our tiles. It didn't take long before Lynn and Carene were sketching away. After much pondering all I could come up with was my famous cow, a doodle I have been amazing family and friends with for years. I tried to concentrate on this one so it would at least be recognizable. As we sketched, Yosiet's wife worked on a clay piece of a city scene in 3D. When Lynn came and stood behind me to have a look at my drawing, I heard a little, almost inaudible gasp. She quietly asked if it was a cow. Carene, who was sitting beside me, and bless her, hadn't asked what the hell I was doing, quietly said, "Oh, that's the cow my mom always drew when I was a little girl." I thought, sometimes children can be so worth it. There I was again, having another profound moment, and the day was early.

Carene's tile was shaping up to show the four seasons while Lynn was making hers into a leaf. I kept looking at mine and thought "No, it doesn't look like something a five-year-old would draw, it's abstract." As we worked, occasionally people wandered into the studio to say hello to Yosiet and visit. A familiar face walked in - it was Mario, the Spanish rap artist I'd met in 2006. He asked if I remembered him and I replied, of course I did. He stayed to chat, all the while practising his English with Lynn. Because all I had been doing was basically drawing a picture onto the clay, Yosiet offered me some hints on how I could improve my tile by getting depth into it. After a little more work, I came to the conclusion I had done about all I could do with my cow, so I washed up.

I had brought some small gifts so I gave them to Yosiet's wife. One of the items Cuban ladies love receiving are bras, so I had included one in the package. When we returned a couple of days later, she was wearing it, probably for my benefit, but at least I knew she liked it.

Real arrived to tell us that it was time to go to Manolo's for lunch so we said good-bye with plans to return in a couple of days.

Jesús had explained beforehand that Mayra cooks for visitors to Muraleando. She charges a sum of money to cover the cost of the food and a little for Muraleando, so he suggested an amount for me to give. As we climbed the stairs to Manolo's, I could smell wonderful aromas coming from inside. Mayra, who has the friendliest blue eyes, greeted us, welcoming us to her home. We were shown where we could wash up and then invited to join Real and Lynn at the table. Real explained we would be dining on *ropa vieja*, which is ripped pork in a tasty broth. Translated, it means old clothes, because it is supposed to resemble old tattered clothes. There was also rice, yucca, a widely used root vegetable in Cuba, plantains and bread. Cubans usually have a plate of fresh fruit on the table and today it was pineapple and guava.

Mayra, along with her mother and sister-in-law were busy scurrying around the kitchen and before long, in walked Manolo. I jumped up to greet him and he hugged me warmly. All the while artists wandered in to say hello. They congregate on the back patio for lunch and a siesta.

I gave them some gifts I had brought, and we all had a nice visit. As the time neared for us to leave, Jesús told me it had been arranged for Manolo's father-in-law to drive us in Manolo's car, and I should give him 6 CUC for gas. I could tell they have a well-run system with everyone doing their bit for Muraleando.

We were dropped at an artist's co-op which sold a variety of goods at reasonable prices. I purchased three metal candle holders, complete with candles, and a framed picture of a Cuban country scene. We'd had a full day so we hailed a taxi, dropped Jesús at his house, and then headed back to the hotel. We wouldn't be seeing him the next day, but made plans for Wednesday.

It was now around five o'clock which is a beautiful time of the day in Cuba, so we freshened up and went to The Veranda to relax over a mojito. While we sat, we watched as a debutant was having her photos taken. Because the grounds of the hotel are so beautiful, it is a common sight to see debutants as well as brides posing for pictures.

When girls turn fifteen in Cuba, they are given a party by their parents to celebrate their debut into society. They dress up in elaborate bride-like dresses, usually rented for the occasion, and have professional photographs taken. The girl today wore a beautiful crystal-encrusted soft pink princess gown and a tiara. As she strolled the grounds, I went and asked if I could take a photo. She turned, posed and smiled beautifully for me.

That night we went to the small nightclub below the restaurant where we had eaten. Some of the tables were full, and ones with a good view of the stage had reserved signs on them. A hostess told us if we didn't mind sitting at the bar, there was plenty of room there. Before long the room began to fill, and it seemed a lot of the crowd knew one another.

Carene's meal wasn't sitting well, so it wasn't long before the girl sitting beside her, who was quite fidgety, began to irritate her. She referred to her as Twitchy then proceeded to tell me how Twitchy erred when she had dressed for the evening. Apparently she was too glittery. I was told when you have glitter on your eyes and nails, you don't wear glittery clothes. A lesson learned.

The entertainment was a man who sang to taped music and sometimes played guitar. He was very good and everyone seemed to be enjoying themselves. He told the odd joke, which unfortunately we didn't understand, but when they say laughter is contagious, they are right.

At one point during his performance he did something that puzzled me. Between songs, just before he took a moment to take a sip of his drink, he poured a small amount onto the floor at his feet. Nothing was said as he did this, but I was curious. When I returned home and began to research different things about Cuba, I came across the following fact about Santería. It is quite common when a bottle of rum is opened for a few drops to be poured onto the floor in the corner of the room as an offering to the gods.

We wouldn't be seeing Jesús today so we took advantage of the pool at the hotel for a relaxing day. We changed into our bathing suits, gathered up some reading material, smeared ourselves with sun tan lotion, (or so I thought), and headed to the pool. Carene found a spot in the sun while I opted for shade under some trees. Getting settled takes some work on my part, so I got busy. I chose a lounge chair and a table to put beside me. A mosquito landed on me so I swatted it, then continued getting settled. After brushing some leaves from my chair, I put my towel on it and sat down. Just as I got comfy another mosquito landed on my foot. With thoughts of malaria and dengue fever in my head, I figured the best plan was to move. I relocated under a palm where Carene joined me, telling me she needed some shade. The sun was very intense even though it was only ten a.m.

I noticed a woman eating a plate full of tomatoes, so when it came time for lunch I inquired about a tomato salad. The waitress told me it wasn't on the menu but she would be happy to bring me a plate of tomatoes. Carene ordered a sandwich and of course, we both needed a mojito. The tomatoes were awesome. You just can't beat the flavour of tomatoes ripened in the hot sun. All they needed was oil, vinegar, and lots of salt and pepper. After ordering another mojito for pool-side, we sat and discussed what to do for the rest of the day.

Back in the room Carene was getting redder by the minute, with me coming up a close second. When I asked her if she had put on sun tan lotion, she sheepishly replied, "A little." I took that to mean she had only put it on her face. My back was quite red and I realized the ten minutes or so when I had sat on the edge of the pool with nothing on my back hadn't been too smart. Carene stated she should have clued in when she put a damp towel over her legs and it felt so good. We laughed saying when Jesús saw us the next day he would think that he had only left us alone for one day and look what happened!

It was too late to do much so we took a walk along the Malecón toward Habana Vieja. It is quite interesting walking the back streets and seeing people going about their everyday lives. Construction workers were finishing up for the day, while some children, dressed in their school uniforms, were returning home. We watched as bags of groceries, tied with a rope, were lifted to upper levels of the tenements. It was a beautiful evening so we walked on the Paseo del Prado and went to the same paladar where Jesús had taken us for lunch our first day. After dinner we found a *bodega* so we could buy some rum to take home. Four bottles of rum and a large bottle of water cost 27 CUC. Could this get any better?

In the morning, Jesús picked us up in a cocotaxi that could hold three passengers. We were going to a cemetery before the day became too hot, and then to the rum and cigar factories. I did wonder why we were going to a cemetery but trusted Jesús, as he hadn't failed me yet.

*Necrópolis Colón is one of the largest cemeteries in the world, occupying an area of 135 acres and with about two million graves. Because of its many sculptures and monuments in different styles – from eclectic to the boldest expressions of contemporary art – the Necrópolis has been proclaimed a national monument.

First, we entered a building where some historic papers and artifacts were on display, and where people can choose simple headstones. We began to walk around and Jesús pointed out graves of interest, telling us the story behind each one. Many of the markers for heroes and martyrs are paid for by collections taken up in their honour.

We came upon a large monument, surrounded by many flowers and a lot of small plaques behind it. It was the tomb of Amelia Goyri de la Hoz.

*Amelia Goyri de la Hoz, or "The Miraculous One", along with her daughter, died in childbirth at the age of twenty-four in 1901. In keeping with the custom of the time, she and the child were buried together, the child at her feet. According to popular legend, a few years later when the tomb was opened she was found intact, holding her baby in her arms. This miracle, and the fact that her bereaved husband went to her tomb every day and never turned his back to it, made Amelia a symbol of motherly love. She became the protector of pregnant women and newborn children, and her tomb is a pilgrimage site for future mothers, who ask for her blessing and leave without turning their back to the tomb.

After Jesús told us the story, he instructed us what to do. We were to knock with the large brass ring attached to the monument, to wake her up, and then stand beside the statue, touch her, and ask for a miracle.

Behind her tomb there were many small plaques thanking Amelia for miracles granted. Another section of her tomb held little houses thanking her for homes. At that time, Cubans could only trade houses, so people would ask for Amelia's help in finding them a home.

Because the cemetery is so large we visited only a small section. Between the many angels surrounding us, and the holiness, I found myself feeling emotional so when I asked Jesús if this was where Fidel would be laid to rest it came out a teary squawk. I told myself to get a grip.

Next we were off to the rum factory. I knew there really wasn't too much to see here but, because Carene had never been, I thought why not? The tour guide was in the middle of a large Spanish-speaking tour so Jesús suggested we go upstairs for tastings until they finished. There, a woman offered us tastes of rum, explaining the different types. One of the samples we tried was sweet rum, sometimes referred to as ladies' rum and I quite liked it. We looked at cigars and couldn't believe how pricey some were. After purchasing some Cuban coffee Jesús arranged a brief tour in English. It came with the usual jokes that every tour guide seems to add to their spiel, but we made sure we laughed.

After leaving the rum factory we were having difficulties getting a taxi, so walked a bit. We passed a butcher's stall containing only a cooler, a counter and a large blackboard on the wall. When a customer shops for meat, the butcher marks it down on the black board, then, when the customer receives his monthly subsidy the bill is paid and the board erased. We came upon a shoemaker who had simply set up shop at the front of a building. Today he was working on a pair of rubber flip-flops, gluing the part that had broken away, and then stitching it back in place. It seemed like a lot of work for flip flops, but in Cuba they repair things until they are beyond repair. The shoemaker had a big smile on his face, seeming to be very happy in his work.

Jesús was finally able to find us a ride, not in a taxi, but rather a truck with an enclosed back holding bench seats down each side. We climbed in and Jesús sat up front with the driver. It was another mode of transportation we would experience because we had a Spanish guide. With the air thick with the smell of diesel, I tried not to choke and went with the experience. We were dropped at the cigar factory with a plan for Jesús to set us up with an English tour, then leave us and pick us up later at the hotel for the concert in Muraleando.

Our guide was a young woman in her twenties and as feisty as they come. The tour was small and we began by stating where we were from, and then went to a room where women sat sorting leaves used for the outside of the cigars. After an explanation of what went on there, a young Australian man asked the guide a question and she decided to tease him a little about not listening. He didn't have a very good sense of humour and told her he was partially deaf in one ear and it wasn't something to joke about. An awkward silence fell over the group but the guide didn't seem to be fazed by his attempt at embarrassing her. Carene, who had spent a year in Australia, commented to me that an Aussie man wouldn't like being teased by a woman, especially a black woman.

The tour continued and was very interesting. We saw where people learn to roll cigars, all the while being supervised. When they have proven themselves, they move upstairs with the professional rollers. The workers are allowed to smoke as many cigars as they want while on the job and are given three a day to take home. They are expected to make a quota every day, depending on the job. When the guide was asked if the workers are penalized if they don't make their quota, she looked puzzled by the question, replying no, this is Cuba, there is no penalty. Once you are given a job in the factory, you do that job at all times. There are people who do nothing other than put labels on the cigars and others who only box product.

The factory employs a large number of people, the majority being women. They work five days a week from seven a.m. until five p.m. and lunch is supplied. As people left the lunch room, they washed their personal utensils before returning to their station. No throwaway utensils here. Music played in the large rooms where people sat working and they are read to in the afternoons. A reader sits at a table with a microphone at the front of the room, first reading the newspaper, *Granma,* and then from a chosen book.

Carene and I were waiting at the front of the hotel to be picked up to go to the concert in Muraleando when a little girl appeared and kissed me on the cheek. It was Jenny, Jesús' daughter, dressed up for the occasion. At the end of the driveway a friend of Jesús who would drive us, and Juan, his brother-in-law, were waiting. Juan was there to film the concert for a documentary he was working on.

As we drove along chatting, I was asked if we had seen any roaches at the hotel and what the food is like. I had been noticing there seemed to be a mystique attached to the hotel and assumed the history and its majestic look had something to do with it.

Arriving in Muraleando, we went directly to Manolo's house. Another couple was already there, sitting in the living room, while the rest of the household ate dinner. The Canadian in me began emerging and I was feeling very intrusive. Their house is always busy, but I just wanted to let them eat in peace, so I went outside. Manolo's house is very near to what they refer to as The Club, which is where the concert would take place, so I was witnessing a flurry of activity. Two young men came and called up to Manolo needing something. He appeared and sent them off with some sort of solvent and a stick with a rag tied on the top. I assumed we were going to see a torch of some sort. Another lady appeared with a young girl in an elaborate dance costume.

When we arrived at The Club a crowd of children were already standing along a yellow tape, keeping them back from the stage. I saw people in costumes in the wings when all of a sudden Irasema appeared in front of me. I had been told she would be participating in the concert and was pleased to see her again. We hugged each other and the tears began to flow. She was busy with the concert but did manage to come over throughout the evening.

The concert began and I could tell we were in for a treat. A Michael Jackson clone performed who had the moon walk down pat. He and his backup group did a remake of the video "Thriller", complete with fake blood, torches, and zombies. MC Mario did some of his rap songs and different dancers performed. The concert ended with a teen-age couple dancing a salsa number.

Manolo introduced Real, telling the audience about her gift to Muraleando that enabled them to make the glass mural. He explained that everyone should take pride in it.

We were invited back to Manolo's for café, and after a short visit we said our good-byes. The artists were all going to the beach the next day to celebrate another successful festival. They had extended an invitation to us, but we had to decline because we had dinner planned at the Lazaros.

Since we hadn't eaten dinner we went to the hotel cafeteria for a bite. With mojitos in hand, and motormouths going full speed, we happily munched away while we talked about the evening. I had been hearing how happy they were that I'd returned and brought Carene with me. These special people had made us feel very welcome.

For our last day with Jesús, we had plans to go back to Yosiet's to paint ceramic tiles with water colour. Jesús wanted to learn more about ceramics, so he was also going to paint a tile.

At Yosiet's we were welcomed and offered café before getting to the task at hand. Yosiet's wife was painting small clay turtles in various colours that would later be taken to different art shows to sell. They are a popular item because they can be sold for a small sum. Another artist arrived and began working on a 3D clay piece. The speed in which he worked was amazing to watch. Yosiet prepared the paints, explaining the different colours and how they work with each other. We were again given a piece of paper to draw what we might put on our tile. I had lots of ideas in my head, but putting them on paper wasn't easy for untalented me. While we worked away, my heart was full as I experienced another one of my Cuban highs. The cat had once again made itself comfortable on my purse, Yosiet had music playing in the background, and I whispered to Carene that this was a pretty cool thing we were experiencing. My tile was even shaping up OK. I was trying to get the idea across that my heart belongs to Cuba. Carene was painting a fancy flower on hers and Jesús was incorporating a fish onto his. Yosiet disappeared then returned with a bowl of mangoes and forks, telling us to dig in. They were delicious and bursting with flavour. When Jesús mentioned that he loved the lyrics of John Lennon's "Imagine", Yosiet put it on and we all sang along. The words seemed to fit this scenario perfectly. I was feeling emotional, partly because the whole Cuban experience had been phenomenal, and partly because it was coming to an end.

In the two days we had spent at Yosiet's we found him to be very sensitive and not afraid to show his emotions. When he talked about *Raku* pottery, which is almost sacred to him, his arms broke out in goose bumps which, he told us, happens when something touches him emotionally. When he explained how his wife had been accepted into art school, and how proud he was of her work, he teared up. His wife smiled proudly and Carene and I came to the conclusion we loved this man.

We finished up and were taking some pictures when Yosiet told us to choose one of the turtles his wife had been painting. We were also given postcards, adorned with pictures and poems by different artists. We said our good-byes promising to return, we hoped, next year.

Jesús said that Manolo had arranged lunch for us with his mother-in-law, Erminda, and Lynn would be joining us. Lynn hadn't gone to the beach and was having a morning to herself in Muraleando. Erminda is the sweetest lady ever, and Jesús assured us she was a wonderful cook. We sat down to one of the best meals I'd ever eaten. There was pork loin, yucca, rice, salad, and a frozen drink made from guava that was incredible. I didn't know how she had cooked the pork, but we couldn't get enough. There was also pineapple and guava on the table and the meal ended with café. While we sat chatting, birds housed in cages in the window, sang merrily. As the time came to leave I couldn't hold back the tears. I just wanted to stay and hug this woman.

We were going to walk around Muraleando to take some photos of different murals, and then Tony, Manolo's father-in-law, would drive us back to the hotel. We came upon Victor, (the tall one), working on the latest mural on the façade of a house. He hadn't gone to the beach with the others as he wanted to finish the project. When Tony pulled up, we said good-bye to Victor and Muraleando, vowing to return.

Jesús presented us with four Churchill cigars, a CD, and a DVD as gifts. I added a bonus in with his last payment, feeling every cent had been worth it. There were teary good-byes among us all with promises to return. Jesús assured us Juan would meet us later at the Lazaros for dinner and to translate.

Back at the Nacional we went and sat at the edge of the rock and ordered mojitos, enjoying our last afternoon in Cuba. I could have sat there forever, but we had a dinner date.

When we pulled up in front of Lazaro's, he and Melina were waiting for us. There was a young boy with them that I hadn't met who gave us both a kiss. We learned he was Lazaro's younger brother, Kmilo. As we made our way up the stairs, Lazaro's grandmother came out to thank me for the gift I had left for her. When we entered the home, the first thing I noticed was how beautifully the table was set. They had obviously gone to a lot of trouble so I was glad we had dressed up for the occasion. Juan had already arrived, so while Dad prepared the meal, we all sat and visited. Having Juan there certainly made it easier to communicate. On the table there were bottles of ice water, a basket of bread with the crusts cut off, a bowl of banana chips and a plate of pineapple and guava. Plates were brought out of the kitchen with chicken and accompanying it was rice, fried plantains, salad and *potaje*. Potaje is a thick soup made from black or red beans, fried garlic, onion, pepper, oregano and cumin that is eaten with or without a bowl of while rice.

Mom, Dad and Melina weren't eating with us, I assumed because they just didn't have room to seat everyone, but they sat and chatted with us while we dined. The meal ended with my favourite Cuban dessert, *flan de huevos,* a Spanish dessert similar to crème caramel, and café.

We talked about The View project and I filled them in on the news of people I was still in touch with. They said how happy the barrio had been that summer and how much the children missed us after we were gone. When we talked about the day the authorities came to their house, I learned something interesting. It seemed the police were afraid we were going to exploit them by taking pictures back to Canada to show how poorly Cuban people live.

Lazaro and Melina brought out their photo albums from the project, proudly showing them to Carene. Both were well-worn, which told me they were treasured. Lazaro stated he wanted to become a photographer and I remembered he did have a good eye.

Even though the family lives simply, the love they share is heartwarming. Mom told me her home isn't fancy, but it seemed like a castle to me. The family escorted us to the street and after lots of hugs and tears we were told that whenever we visit Cuba we have a home with them.

I asked Juan to join Carene and me for a drink so I could pay him. He found a little outdoor café and we ordered beer. As we sat talking we learned about his life and we told him about ours. We all agreed that the Lazaros were good people.

Back at the hotel, we found a phone message waiting. Carene listened and heard a woman speaking slowly in Spanish. After we listened a few times, we figured out that it was Consuelo de la Angelos, the woman we'd met on the street with Jesús, asking if we were coming to her house. I hadn't realized we had made a firm date and felt terrible about the mix-up. I guess when Cubans tell you to drop by, they really mean it. I called Jesús and asked him to call her and make our apologies.

My dreams that night were about what I would take to Cuba the next time I visit. Number one on my list was a digital camera for Lazaro.

After breakfast, we went to The Veranda for one last café. I found myself feeling very sad to be leaving this beautiful country, but knew I'd be back.

Bonnie Martin

Observations and Reflections - 2008

My first reflection is on Fidel Castro. I don't know a lot about him, but love reading and learning as much as I can. One thing I find truly amazing is that a man of eighty-two, who had been on his death bed two years previously, still writes long articles called "Reflections of Fidel" for Cuba's national newspaper, Granma. People have different opinions about him, but mine is that he has made life better in Cuba for many, and they love him.

The people of Cuba really are one of a kind. Just being around them makes you smile, because that's usually what they are doing. The joy they get out of life is something we could all learn from. They are warm and kind with each other, as well as strangers.

The way the Cuban people always greet each other is something I have come to love. Men shake hands, and when greeting a female, they kiss on the cheek. Women, as well as children, kiss each other in the same way.

In Canada, drivers honk their horns, usually to tell someone to get out of the way. In Cuba, drivers honk their horns constantly, but they do it to warn pedestrians and other drivers that they are coming.

In most homes, the main sitting room usually contains two rocking chairs in a place of importance. When a guest arrives they are offered a seat, no matter who might be sitting in the chair.

In Cuba, I don't think you could ever intrude on anyone. When we arrived unannounced at the Lazaros our first night, we were invited in without hesitation. Grandma had been watching TV, and big brother was just getting out of the shower, wearing only a towel. We were both welcomed warmly as if they had been expecting us.

The last thing I'd like to reflect upon is karma, or as I have come to believe, the angels in my life. It was through a casual conversation with Carene regarding travel, and me wanting to re-visit Cuba, that the trip was first talked about. The date to go depended on some previous plans of Carene's, but the week we chose ended up being a perfect time to visit.

If Jesús hadn't approached me the last day we were together in 2006 and given me his card, this holiday would have been completely different, as would all the experiences that came afterward.

Section Three

April 2009

Bonnie Martin

Childrens workshop, Muraleando – 2009

My Love Affair with Cuba

People You'll Meet

Carlos

Carlos is a friend of Jesús who he uses as a driver for tourists. He is a retired navy man, and for that reason owns a car. Very few people in Cuba own cars, but ex-military men are some of the fortunate ones able to purchase a used car at a good price.

Debbie Danelley - Artist

Debbie is an artist from Winnipeg who travels to Cuba every year to volunteer in Muraleando. She leads workshops for children as part of the Muraleando Community Project.

Chapter Four

Cuba had become very special to me, so it didn't take me long to realize I wanted to return. Carene also fell in love with the country in 2008, so when I asked her if she would like to visit again, she readily agreed. We returned in April, pretty much the same time we visited the previous year, which enabled us to attend the Muraleando festival. Our adventure continued, seeing old friends and making new ones.

We were staying at the Hotel Nacional again, and settled right in, beginning our holiday the way we had last year, by going out to the rock overlooking the water, and ordering mojitos. One of the nice things about return visits is doing familiar things that you enjoy.

As pre-arranged, Jesús met us the next morning to take us to Muraleando. He had a car waiting with a driver, Carlos. Jesús' wife Maria, and his daughter, Jenny, were also in the car and would accompany us to Muraleando. When we entered the barrio we stopped to see the newest mural that had just been completed. It was beautiful with a soft golden background and painted in muted but happy colours. It was easy to pick out the different artists' contributions in the mural - Victor's familiar large-eyed girl, Jesús' fish, Manolo's women with flowers in their hair and Nivia's work depicting children. Other images had been painted by other artists, one being Debbie, a guest artist from Winnipeg, who we would meet later. Even a hydro pole beside the mural had been painted to resemble a totem pole.

On Manolo's roof-top, a children's workshop was in progress. It was being run by Debbie, with the help of Nivia, Mayra and some mothers from the barrio.

Before going up to the roof, we were greeted by different people, some familiar and some not. When I saw Mario, I was anxious to speak with him. Just before leaving for Cuba I had learned that his two-year-old daughter had lost her second eye to cancer, and was now completely blind. I tried to hold my emotions in check while he assured me his daughter was recuperating nicely in hospital and receiving very good care.

We climbed the steep metal stairs leading to Manolo's rooftop studio and found it buzzing with activity. We were briefly introduced to Debbie as well as a young man from Germany, who was in Cuba as part of his German military obligation. The children were all sitting, working away, and I could tell they were right into the project. They had taken old books that were no longer useable and turned them into beautiful works of art. One boy's was a ship, complete with masts and flags. Others had beads, feathers and sparkles added to pictures they had coloured on the pages. As the children finished, they tidied up where they had been working, then made their way to an old hairdressing sink to wash up. This was done without prodding from an adult, which led me to the conclusion that Cuban children are very mature for their age. They were then taken one at a time to a table where Debbie took a picture of them with their work.

Nivia appeared carrying a bucket of water, a ladle and some plastic glasses. The bucket had been set in a freezer so the water was ice cold. As they waited patiently, she ladled out water for each of them.

There was going to be a party for the children, so Nivia and Mayra were scurrying around. Cuban people love a party and any excuse for one will do. A table was brought up and set with a big cake in the centre, along with plates of finger food. Large bottles of soda also decorated the table and there was orange drink for the children. When a table is set for an occasion, quite often it will be decorated with a fancy cake as well as bottles of soda. Fancy decorated cakes are usually served, be it a large or small event, and it is a common sight to see people in the streets carrying decorated cakes home. Because paper products are expensive, they are carried without a box.

Debbie had been taken to the street on some false premise so they could surprise her later with a gift. When the sign was given that she was coming, a cheer rang out. Her face showed surprise and she began to cry. The people in Cuba heap so much love on guests, I could relate to her tears. Manolo said a few words thanking Debbie and told the children how special her visit was.

It was now time for the party to begin. The children were served first, each receiving a plate containing a large piece of cake, as well as other various treats. When they finished eating, a girl of about nine stood and recited a poem by José Martí, one of Cuba's national heroes. After her, another girl stood and recited a poem she had written. I felt I was in the midst of some very young intellectuals.

At the end of the Muraleando festival the artists reward themselves for all of their hard work with either a day at the beach or a picnic in Parque Lenin. This year they were going to Parque Lenin and Carene and I were invited to join them for a day of fun.

Jesús, Maria, Jenny, Carene and I left telling everyone we would see them Thursday. We were going to visit Yosiet and his family, but found no one home, so we walked to find a taxi. The one that pulled over for us was one of the most unique vehicles I had ever seen. It was an old Lada that had been "stretched". They had taken the back from one Lada, and the front from another, then welded them together to make a taxi with two back seats. I could add this to my list of unusual modes of transport in Cuba. It never ceases to amaze me how inventive they are. We dropped Maria and Jenny at a bus stop then Jesús, Carene and I headed toward Old Havana to continue our day.

While we walked around Old Havana taking in the sights and sounds, we came upon a band, followed by a group of dancers, parading through the narrow streets. As they walked and danced, people joined, dancing and clapping while following them. Jesús was getting right into it so we did the same. We all ended up in Plaza de Armas and there everyone gathered around while the dancing continued at a frenzied pace. With the dancers in costume, we wondered how they could keep going in the heat. Plaza de Armas did offer shade, but the temperature was still in the nineties. The group was from the University of Havana, and had a woman in the centre directing them. As I craned my neck to look toward the other end of the group, I could see what I thought was an enthusiastic onlooker dancing with them. She was dressed in a very short mini skirt, thigh-high white boots, and was shaking her booty

My Love Affair with Cuba

big time. When she danced her way to our end, I realized she was a transvestite, and she was fabulous. Cuba is very liberal in their attitude toward sex and the like, generally taking the approach, "each to his own, and love thy fellow man." How refreshing it was not to have someone jeering insults and wanting to harm her. It was well over an hour from the time we joined them in the street, until they left the plaza, still dancing. I was exhausted just watching them.

Since there were still a lot of things I hadn't yet seen in Havana, I told Jesús of places we would like to visit. He hired Carlos to drive us and came up with a plan. First we visited Finca La Vigía, Ernest Hemingway's villa, located at San Francisco de Paula, on the outskirts of Havana.

*Ernest Hemingway first visited Cuba in 1932 and fell in love with it. He moved to the island in 1939 and resided in the Ambos Mundos hotel in Old Havana. It was after he decided to stay on that he found the villa, Finca La Vigía, at San Francisco de Paula, where he could write. He lived there on and off for twenty years, returning to the USA in 1960, a year before his suicide.

Finca La Vigía is a beautiful spot that makes you realize why Hemingway loved Cuba so. It has been carefully restored, and even though you can't go inside, it is fitted with large windows enabling you to see everything. There are women in each room who, for a few pesos, will take photos for you. The grounds are lush with an abundance of tropical plants and many large trees. Hemingway's fishing boat, the Pilar, sits on display in a specially built pavilion. Jesús pointed out a row of about five small graves with headstones with the names of some of his dogs. He told us Batista's men had killed them for some reason.

Bonnie Martin

A Moment in Time - Cubans being Cubans

While visiting Finca La Vigía, I witnessed two instances of Cuban people looking out for one another. When we were paying our entry fee at the gate, Jesús quietly told me not to pay the extra fee that would enable me to take pictures, but instead, to give it directly to the ladies in the villa. The next instance touched my heart greatly. As we were looking in the windows, a Cuban couple with two children were in front of us. While the guide explained things, the mother was taking notes. Jesús overheard them tell the guide they were there because their son was doing a school project on Hemingway, but since they had used all their money for the bus ride there, and the entry fee, they didn't have money left to take pictures. The guide, without hesitation, took their camera and began snapping away. It was not only an example of how strong the family unit is in Cuba, but also how Cuban people will help each other.

Our next stop was the Castillo del Morro, a huge fortress on Havana harbour, one of the many Castillos throughout Cuba.

*Construction on Castillo del Morro began in 1589 at the request of the governor, Juan de Texeda. The original lighthouse on the *morrillo,* the highest point of the hill, was rebuilt several times before the current one in 1845. It is made entirely of stone, and has its original lamp, the rays of which can be seen for twenty miles. Today the Castillo del Morro is open to visitors as the Parque Histórico-Militar.

On the day we visited, an art exhibition was taking place, with artists from all over the world displaying their work. It was very interesting with many unique displays. Even though Jesús was doing his best to explain the meanings of the different exhibits, I knew there was a lot we missed because of our lack of Spanish.

Because Carlos had dropped us there, we had to find our own way back to Havana. Jesús' original plan was to take a ferry but, because the exhibition was so large and had taken longer than anticipated, he thought in the interest of time we would take a taxi. Finding a taxi in Havana when you are away from main tourist areas can be quite challenging and we were about to witness an instance where having a guide is well worth the money. We walked to a parking lot where some taxis sat with a couple of drivers killing time. Jesús spoke to one and my impression was that he couldn't take us. We walked away and when we came upon a small group of black and white goats with some very cute kids, we stopped to take some pictures. There was a faint honk and Jesús said, "Here is our hidden taxi." I didn't ask questions - just climbed in.

The taxi dropped us near the Prado and Jesús said we would have lunch in a paladar he was familiar with. The owner told us today she was serving pork or fish. There was a touch of Creole in the cooking that added to the flavour. Cubans don't use a lot of spice in their cooking, probably because of the cost, so when some is added it makes a nice change.

We had plans to visit the Lazaro's. I had brought a camera for Lazaro and couldn't wait to give it to him. On our last trip, when we had dinner at his home, he proudly showed Carene his hand-made photo album from 2006 and told us he wanted to become a photographer. That started the wheels turning in my head. I purchased a used Minolta digital camera from a trusted local camera shop, adding a large memory and lots of batteries. Because it was used, it came with a camera bag and some other attachments. My husband copied the Spanish version of the manual so Lazaro would be set up nicely. Carene had orders to take pictures while I was giving Lazaro the camera.

When we pulled up in a taxi, Lazaro and Juan were waiting for us. After hugs and kisses, as we began to climb the stairs, Lazaro's grandmother and his older brother came out of their apartment to greet us. We climbed the steep, narrow stairs leading to Larazo's home and I tackled them like an old pro. When we reached the roof, Mom and Melina were waiting for us and introduced us to Lazaro's girlfriend, Yoena. Upon entering the home I could see they had renovated. The walls in the main room, previously Styrofoam panels joined together with wire, were now covered with wood panels. Shelves had been added to display pictures and other ornaments, and a new light fixture and sofa completed the look. When I complimented them, Mom proudly told me Lazaro had done the work the previous winter.

We were offered ice water then Lazaro and Yoena got busy in the kitchen making café. I began passing out gifts to everyone but since Lazaro was busy his would have to wait. Little brother came in to show Carene his baby rabbit. He took the rabbit out of the cage, plopped it on her shoulder, and told her it would just sit there, and he was right, it did. By now I was so dizzy with excitement I was actually shaking. When Lazaro was ready, I began the presentation of the camera and right away the tears came. Juan was saying how nice this was and I could hardly speak. I heard Carene behind me quietly saying, "Bonnie, settle down!" My tears had turned into a full-on body-racking sob – I actually broke – and the more I cried the tighter Lazaro held me while he cried. I'll never forget the experience, and when I hear the adage, "It's better to give than to receive", I relate totally.

While we sat visiting, the topic of Melina's fifteenth birthday came up. Mom told us she only had one more year to wait, and because we are family, of course we would be invited. Whenever I hear things like that a warm feeling comes over me, and I vowed, if at all possible, I'd be there.

Mom kept complimenting Carene on her new haircut and colour, saying she particularly liked the strip of red she had in it. I would learn more about that the next night when the family would be my guests for a dinner out.

Today would be another day of touring with Jesús and Carlos. This was the third time I had been a passenger in Carlos' car and had begun to notice that he drove like a madman, no worse than most Cuban drivers, but I was nervous.

A Moment In Time - A traffic stop

We hadn't gone very far when a motorcycle cop who was sitting on the side of the Malecón motioned for us to pull over. Just before Carlos hopped out he grabbed some papers from his sun visor before making his way back to the policeman. Jesús told us the papers were his navy identification papers stating he was a retired officer. Military and navy people are greatly respected in Cuba, so Carlos thought showing his papers might help with the situation. Apparently it worked and he returned with only a warning and orders to slow down. Because everyone in Cuba is basically equal, you don't have someone with a little authority letting it go to their heads and abusing their power.

We travelled west toward Miramar, with Jesús pointing out various buildings and hospitals, explaining that in Cuba many hospitals are specialized. One hospital will deal only with pregnant women, while another might deal with eye cataracts.

*Miramar is the most elegant part of Havana – as it was before the Revolution, when the city's richest inhabitants lived here. Life in this quarter revolves around the busy Avenida 5, a broad tree-lined avenue boasting a number of luxury hotels. On both sides of the boulevard are large, imposing mansions built in the early 20th century and many Art Deco and eclectic-style houses, most of which were abandoned by their owners after Fidel Castro took power. The Cuban government has turned many of these buildings into ministries, embassies and even orphanages.

Continuing on we stopped at the fishing village of Cojímar, Marina Hemingway and the home and studio of José Fuster.

*Cojímar was once inhabited only by fishermen but now there are many elderly people, including writers and artists, who have chosen to leave the capital for a more peaceful life. In the 1950s Cojímar is where Ernest Hemingway spent a lot of his time. Many of the local fishermen were his friends, and he liked to play dominoes and drink rum while listening to their stories. He made this village the setting for his famous novel *The Old Man and the Sea* and Cojímar is where his fishing boat *Pilar* was once moored.

Marina Hemingway is where the Ernest Hemingway International Marlin Fishing Tournament is held every year in May. It is a competition reserved for expert marlin fishermen. Jesús told us a story of when Fidel Castro took part in the tournament and caught a huge fish. As it was said, Castro had some of his men under water to make sure the biggest fish got onto the right hook, Castro's. I imagine it is probably an old fishing yarn but the Cubans seem to think it funny.

*José Fuster

José Fuster resides in the village of Jaimanitas where he also has his studio. He paints, engraves and sketches and is also one of Cuba's most original ceramists. He began his artistic career in 1961, at the age of fourteen, when he went to the Sierra Maestra to teach in the Literacy Campaign. He studied at the Art Instructors School from 1963 to 1965. He then started working as a ceramist at the Cubanacan Ceramics Workshop in Havana in 1966. He has participated in contests, exhibits, and art symposia in Cuba and around the world. The artist is spending some of his earnings to improve his neighbours' homes. He also organizes friends to improve the quality of life in a city where few are truly starving, but most scrimp and scrape to survive. For those without access to dollars, salaries are meagre and home repairs are a luxury. This is where Fuster helps. He is successful and happy to share his good fortune.

Upon entering Fuster's property we were met with a blaze of colour. On the ground level there was a pool, an outdoor bar, and sculptures, while the walls were covered in mosaics and hand-painted ceramic tiles. We climbed a staircase, also covered with painted ceramic tiles, to find the artist's studio. It held paintings and tiles along with other various objects all painted in his unique style. He had taken old vinyl records and empty rum bottles and painted them, turning them into works of art. Another set of stairs led to the roof where there were more sculptures, all done in mosaics. He had even covered his water tanks and parts of the roof below in mosaics. It was hard to imagine how many hours it had taken to create it all. While we wandered around we were met by Fuster's grown son who told us the artist wasn't home but to feel free to look around. I purchased a painted rum bottle and, just as we were leaving, the artist returned home, so I managed to have my picture taken with him and my purchased work of art.

Since we were in the vicinity, we dropped in on Jesús' older sister and her family. Jesús greeted her with much love and tenderness, all the while telling us how she had helped raise the younger children in the family, being a great help to their mother while she worked. He showed us around the home, pointing out the new refrigerator the state had provided, to replace the old inefficient one. We went out to the back patio, and when we turned to climb the metal stairs leading to the upper floor, we were introduced to the house pig. Housed behind the kitchen in a concrete stall, the pig was quite happy in his cool, shady and clean (well, as clean as a pig sty can be) home. Upstairs, we were introduced to Jesús' niece and her husband, a policeman. He was renovating the attached house next door, owned by seasonal people, to earn a little extra money for the family. I saw Jesús slip his niece some money, and when I mentioned it to Carene later, she told me she had seen him do the same with his sister. It was another example of the strong family bond in Cuba which I would witness many more times.

We told Jesús we would be happy to call it a day and go back to the hotel for some pool time. We said our good-byes telling him we would see him Thursday for our day in Parque Lenin.

Thinking it would be a good time to buy our rum, we went in search of the store where we had purchased it the previous year. As we were trying to decide what kind we wanted, a Cuban gentleman came to our aid. He and his lady friend were standing at the counter enjoying a drink of rum and, because he spoke English, he knew he could be of help. We purchased five bottles for a grand total of 55 CUC. We thanked the gentleman, shook his hand, and left to find a taxi. We lucked into a 3 CUC ride in an old Lada that belonged in the junk yard. I can't believe some of these cars still run, especially ones that are literally falling apart like this one was. I was waiting for it to make one last cough, then die, with me sitting inside.

We had arranged to meet Juan and the Lazaros at a paladar for dinner, so we got dressed up and took a taxi. We were all seated at a long table and with Juan's help we began to chat. I thought I heard Mom say something to Carene about loving the band AC/DC and learned that in her younger days she had been into heavy metal music and dressing "Goth". She said she used to have hair the colour of Carene's, which was black at the time, and fingernails to match. Now I knew why she kept complimenting Carene on her hair colour the previous night.

Lazaro had brought his new camera and showed me pictures he had taken of the family before they left home. He seemed to be very comfortable with it, and the quality of the pictures was good. I was pleased, knowing the camera had been a good idea.

After a great meal, it was time to say our good-byes. Down on the street, we lingered, none of us wanting the evening to end. While we spent our last few minutes with each other, I stood back observing. It was then I saw something occur that touched my heart. Melina, fourteen at the time, reached out and took her older brother's hand and held it. I was witnessing pure love between a brother and sister.

Big brother told Lazaro he would like him to take not one, but two pictures of him with Carene and I came to the conclusion he was a little smitten with her. He is quite shy so Carene gladly accommodated him. Lazaro took some more pictures and before long tears began to flow on everyone's part. After lengthy good-byes and promises to see them next year, they began to walk away while we stood watching. Lazaro stopped, turned and came back for one last hug from me which gave me a warm, mushy feeling in my stomach. We said good-bye to Juan until tomorrow then walked back to the hotel talking about how wonderful the evening had been.

Chapter Five

This day would come to be known as Adventure Day. We were going to the province of Pinar del Río in western Cuba. Juan would be our guide and Carlos, our driver. The highway leading to Pinar del Río is a four-lane divided one, and a good road. There were many people hitchhiking along the highway, receiving lifts in all sorts of vehicles, from cars, trucks, and horse-drawn carts, to the back of empty dump trucks. I like the Cuban way of helping each other to get where they are going, and the system seems to work for them.

As we travelled along, the landscape changed to fields of tobacco, sugar cane and rice paddies. Farmers were ploughing their fields with oxen and everyone seemed to be busy. When we made a pit stop to gas up, I should have clued in to why we needed gas so soon, but I was too busy checking out the surroundings, and a washroom break was appreciated. I had expected the washroom facilities along the way would be somewhat lacking but I was wrong. Everything was very clean and the attached snack bar offered a good choice of food. Cuba not only appreciates the tourist dollar and tries to accommodate, but also makes travelling a nice experience for the local people.

We turned off the highway and started passing through small villages. The road began to climb with a lot of curves, and a light rain had begun to fall. Carlos was driving a little fast for my liking, and Carene noticed my nervousness. She suggested that instead of looking out the front window, I look out the side, but when I did, all I saw was a sheer drop beside me with no guard rail in sight.

We were now in the area of the Sierra del Rosario and Sierra de Organos ranges. Because they are only six hundred metres above sea level, these hills aren't high enough to be called mountains, but they do create a breathtaking landscape. We went to a lookout with a spectacular view of a two-mile-wide valley and, as we travelled around the valley, beauty was everywhere. Gigantic limestone formations, called *mogotes* dotted the landscape and all around were thatch-roofed storehouses used for drying tobacco.

*Mogotes are among the most ancient rocks in Cuba, and all that remains of what was once a limestone plateau. Mogotes generally have only a thin covering of soil, but those in the Sierra de los Organos are covered with thick vegetation.

Juan had told me we would be visiting some caves called Palenque de los Cimarrones, but with me being a bit claustrophobic, I had said perhaps I would skip them. He said they really shouldn't be missed, so I relented. At the entrance to the caves there was a snack bar and some tables, so before our tour we indulged in some sort of tropical drink. In the evenings, music is played there, and we could see large speakers around the edge of the area. I couldn't help but think that the sound bouncing off all the rock in the valley must really be something.

Our tour began with a guide, carrying a lantern, leading the way. I was directly behind him and, as is the case with most tours, there was the tour joke. The lantern went out and it was now pitch black. I heard the guide say, "I seem to be having trouble with my light." Stopped dead in my tracks, I was thinking, THIS IS JUST GREAT! The lantern came back on, the joke was over, and after they all had their chuckle we continued on our way.

We came upon a spectacular cave, once a refuge for runaway African slaves. At a spot made to resemble a camp, some Afro Cubans in costume performed a short dance while a drummer played, representing part of their history. We then were taken in a small motor boat up the underground San Vicente River for about a quarter of a mile. The formations made by the stalactites were incredible and the man operating the boat pointed out various shapes that looked like different animals. I felt quite comfortable in the caves as there was plenty of head room so I was glad I had taken Juan's advice.

Not far from the caves is the world's largest mural, Mural de la Prehistoria.

*On the face of a mogote, the Cuban painter Leovigildo Gonzalez, a pupil of the famous Mexican artist Diego Rivera, painted the history of evolution. This took place from 1959 – 1962. The mural, which was restored in 1980, makes use of the cracks in the rock to create special effects of light and colour.

We were now headed to the town of Viñales, a lovely town with a feeling of peacefulness.

*Viñales economy has always been based on agriculture and is now the subject of government protection as an example of a perfectly preserved Colonial settlement. This means when residents want to improve their house they must adhere to strict rules. The main street is lined with many Colonial houses with characteristic arcades, which make useful shelters from the hot sun and sudden violent tropical rainstorms.

**Casa Particulares*, or *casas*, are private homes licenced by the state to rent out rooms. When you rent your room the owner will request a passport or some identification as they are obliged by law to register your personal data with the Immigration Police. The taxes paid for room rental in the casa particulares are used by local authorities to build homes for young couples.

Viñales is a popular destination for visitors to Cuba who mainly stay in one of the many casas located there. We stopped in at one that Juan had dealt with in the past, so he could say hello to the owner, Purry. She invited us in and led us to a covered arcade at the back of the house where she and another woman had been sitting and relaxing, waiting for the rain to pass. We were offered a chair and asked if we would like café. Purry started apologizing about some puddles on the floor from the rain and she couldn't get them mopped up fast enough.

There was a new dining area beyond the arcade, also under cover. This last small area had been added recently, and apparently Purry had to jump through some hoops for it to be allowed. We were asked to sit down to have our café. It was brought out in a small flask and served in demitasse cups with tiny silver spoons. Some cats wandered around, and beside us was a cage holding a chicken with her day-old chicks. Because the chicks were so small, they kept getting out through the holes in the chicken wire, so Carene spent the next few minutes helping Purry get them back where they belonged.

While we enjoyed our café and visit I decided that I really had to come back and spend some time in Viñales.

There is a botanical garden in Viñales that Juan wanted us to see. When we entered the garden, right away I could see that the owners were followers of Santería. A wrought iron fence surrounding the garden had heads of dolls, some with hair and some bald, attached to it. I didn't know what they signified, but when Carene turned and asked me, "What's with the heads?" I had to smile. We were met by a tall, lanky woman who told Juan she would take us through the garden. She said that two sisters had owned the garden since 1919, but sadly, one of them had passed away twenty-five days ago.

The tour began with the guide pointing out different plants, telling Juan their names, which he then relayed to us. She pointed out some of the devastation left from hurricane Ike which struck Cuba in the fall of 2008. The red earth path that wound through the garden was packed down as hard as concrete. A dog joined us and, while herding us, he picked an egg up in his mouth and gently carried it to a tree where he plopped it down in a safe spot, perhaps for a snack later on.

The guide told us that on the day of the deceased sister's funeral they had carried her body through her beloved garden one last time. I now had a lump in my throat the size of the egg the dog had been carrying, and was trying to keep my composure. Carene, who was walking right in front of me heard me sniffling but said nothing.

When the tour finished, we were asked to go into the house to meet the surviving sister and have our picture taken with her.

A Moment In Time - No words needed

The small parlour at the front of the house was crowded with chairs and a settee, all with crocheted doilies on the backs and arms. There were two throne-like chairs sitting side by side with the surviving sister sitting in one, and a large poster-sized photo of the deceased sister hung behind the other. We were introduced to the sister who was dressed immaculately and wore a shawl over her shoulders. She looked so sad my heart was breaking. When I asked Juan to convey our condolences, I could barely speak without choking. As he did, I saw a single tear trickle down her face and it was all I could do to keep from falling apart. I touched her face, and even though we couldn't communicate with words, I knew that she understood the compassion I was feeling for her.

As we left, I had tissues out and was trying to get my act together. We met a lady at the gate, waiting to enter the garden with a look of curiosity on her face, probably wondering what on earth had happened inside to cause my crying. Walking up the street, behind Juan and Carene, I decided a full-on nose blow was needed. Well, I'm sure they heard the echo all over the valley. I could see Juan turn to Carene, and while he was trying to keep a straight face himself told her, "Don't laugh." It might seem unfeeling but wasn't really, and the chuckle we had at my expense was what I needed.

Carlos had told Juan he would wait for us by the town square but, as we walked up the street we couldn't see him or his car. We had been gone for quite some time so Juan was wondering out loud if we had lost him. We found him parked around the corner from the square with the car up on a jack.

The next series of events were a perfect example of what can happen when you don't speak the language and are relying on someone else to take you where you want to go. It's called being clued out, and clued out we were. Juan had told me we would be having lunch at a hotel, but on the way there Carlos pulled over in front of a house. Juan got out and went inside, and when he returned he said something to Carlos. We drove about a half mile out of town and turned into a small hotel complex. Juan told Carene and me to go and have lunch while they went back to Viñales to have the tire repaired. He said to relax, have lunch, and they would pick us up later. When we entered the hotel and stated we would like lunch, a smiling gentleman told us since it was four o'clock we were too late, but we could sit by the pool and have sandwiches and drinks. We walked out back and I breathed a silent sigh of relief. There was a lovely pool and patio area overlooking the valley and the town of Viñales below. We pretty much had the place to ourselves so we ordered chicken sandwiches and mojitos and settled in. It was a beautiful, quiet spot with a marvellous view. There was a scattering of houses with laundry gently blowing in the breeze in the valley, while birds swooped, riding the air currents. The temperature was perfect, the sandwiches tasty, and the mojitos refreshing. I was trying to forget about the car trouble and the trip back to Havana. After sitting for quite some time and drinking our fill, we wandered out front to look around and before long Juan and Carlos arrived, telling us they not only had one flat tire, but four. It all seemed very strange to me but I had long ago stopped trying to figure out things in Cuba.

We began our drive home and my calculations had us not getting back to Havana until around seven-thirty. I think Carlos wanted to make up for lost time because he was driving fast, and I was getting nervous again. At a crossroad in a small village, we came upon a very bad accident. A small car had crashed into a large truck and the car was a mangled mess. People were carrying an injured man away from the wreckage and, by the look of things I thought the accident might have taken his life. I had a sick feeling in the pit of my stomach, and hoped that seeing this accident would slow Carlos down a little.

We drove along with everyone quiet and lost in thought. My nerves were shot, and I'd had my fill of the gas fumes that had been hanging in the air all day. A little later, I saw Carlos give Juan's leg a tap, and soon after, Carene turned to me and said quietly, "We are about to run out of gas." From where she was sitting, she had seen the warning light come on. We were on the highway in the middle of nowhere and running out of gas was the last thing I wanted to happen.

A few miles up the road we came upon the rest stop we had been at that morning, but it was on the other side of the divided highway. Carlos pulled over, opened his trunk, and got out an old plastic juice container that passed for his gas can. He trotted across the highway, and Juan being a true Cuban, acted like this was an everyday occurrence. Then I thought, "This is an everyday occurrence to them." Soon we were on our way again, and now the fumes were even thicker than before. As we drove, me in my own private fog, I finally figured it all out. The gas tank had a hole in it! That's why we had to stop for gas so soon after leaving Havana, and why I'd been smelling fumes all day. It might take me a while to figure things out, but eventually I do.

It was early evening when we entered the hotel and were met with people dressed up, ready for the evening. I'm sure some of them wondered about the two of us, looking dishevelled and absolutely reeking of gasoline. We were tired and dirty, but also hungry, so we freshened up just enough to make ourselves presentable, and went downstairs for a bite to eat. While we noshed and re-lived the events of the day, all we could do was laugh. With me being high on gas fumes, I'm afraid everything seemed funny. Back in the room it was time for my long-awaited shower and nothing had ever felt better.

Chapter Six

Al, a friend from Port Elgin, had listened to me rave about Cuba, so he decided he would take a trip there. He was staying at the Hotel Lido and we had arranged for me to call him on the date of his arrival.

We made a plan to meet at the Hotel Nacional the following morning, then we would take him to Muraleando. I had arranged everything with Juan because Jesús would be working on a project in Muraleando that day. I knew everyone was busy and I didn't want to bother anyone. My intention was to walk around Muraleando with Al, show him some murals, and then visit Yosiet.

The taxi dropped us in front of Manolo's house and he was there working on something. After greeting us, he left briefly, went upstairs to his house, then came and told us to go up for café. I learned, when you show up outside someone's home in Cuba, they don't ask why you are there, they ask you in. The Canadian in me was making me feel uncomfortable as I didn't want to disturb anyone by showing up unannounced. I reminded myself this was Cuba, so up to Manolo's the four of us went. Mayra and her mother were there and it was plain to see they were busy, probably preparing for tomorrow's day in Parque Lenin but, when company arrives, everything stops. We were invited to sit down and offered café. While we were visiting, Nivia and Victor (the older one) arrived, telling us they had arranged something for us. I assumed Manolo had asked them to do it, but I just went along. They said a few of the artists, along with three students from Canada were working on a mural in the school's library. Nivia said that Victor (the tall one) was there, and since we hadn't seen him yet, we should go.

It is quite rare to be allowed into schools in Cuba. Some well-meaning tourists take school supplies when they visit and like to take them to the schools. The supplies are very much appreciated but the school authorities don't want the students being disturbed with tourists traipsing through.

We walked the short distance to the school and by now Jesús and another man, dressed up and carrying a briefcase, had joined us. Jesús explained the man was a promoter for Muraleando, which made me realize I was still a long way from figuring out how everything worked there. Victor (the tall one) greeted us with his usual laugh and I reached way up for a hug. We chatted while they explained what they were doing, but I knew they were busy so we let them get on with their work, saying we would see them all tomorrow in Parque Lenin.

We left to go to Yosiet's with Jesús and the promoter joining us, so we numbered six. When we arrived at Yosiet's Jesús shouted his name and out he came with his big smile. After greetings and introductions he of course invited us in. I can't imagine six people dropping in on someone in Canada on a weekday morning and being welcomed, but again, this was Cuba. The first thing Yosiet did was offer us café. Because I thought I'd had enough café, I declined. What I didn't know was, if you decline café, you're given rum. Well, here it was, eleven-thirty a.m. and I was drinking rum neat, telling myself I was just "going with the flow". Café was brought out and served from a small pot and poured into matching demitasse cups, all made by Yosiet. It was a beautiful set so I made a mental note that next year I would purchase one from him.

Yosiet scurried away again then re-appeared with the two ceramic tiles Carene and I had painted in his studio. He had fired them and then mounted them in frames he had made. As he presented them to us as gifts his wife watched, smiling. We were both touched by the gesture of friendship and appreciated the effort that had gone into it.

While putting gifts together for Cuba, I had come up with the idea to take some Blue Mountain Pottery for Yosiet. I printed some history about it, and as Jesús translated, I explained that Blue Mountain Pottery, no longer made, came from Collingwood, Ontario, a town near my home. Yosiet's eyes filled and I could see his arms had goose bumps, so I knew my idea had been a good one.

We were all milling about chatting, while showing Al some of Yosiet's work. I was trying to get the rum into me and Carene was puffing away on a Cuban cigarette Yosiet had given her. He disappeared yet again, and returned with two pieces of his Raku pottery as another gift for us. He gave me mine, which I accepted graciously, and then he headed toward Carene with hers. She was standing a distance from me so hadn't seen him give me mine. When he presented a piece to her, she responded with a nonchalant *gracias*. I couldn't believe my eyes, and promptly went and asked her what on earth was wrong with her. She looked at me dumbfounded and replied, "I thought he was giving me an ash tray for my ciggy." She glanced around quickly, dumped out the ash, and went and thanked Yosiet properly. I was just glad he hadn't seen her use his precious Raku for an ash tray.

Jesús was gabbing away with Al and it looked like some business was taking place. Al had asked him if he could help locate someone he had met on the way to Cuba, so Jesús, being the business man he is, was forming a plan. He arranged for Juan to take Al to try to find his friend the next day.

I finally got the rum into me, so telling Yosiet and his wife that we would see them tomorrow in Parque Lenin, we left to find a taxi and have lunch. We were dropped near the Prado and Juan suggested a paladar that serves great fish. I asked him to join us but he politely declined. This would be the last we would see him this visit, so Carene and I thanked him for everything, and said our good-byes until next year.

After a nice relaxing lunch with Al, we said good-bye to him, telling him we would see him back in Port Elgin. There were lots of things we thought about doing, but in the end decided we could use some pool time at the hotel. After all, this was a holiday.

After some time at the pool, I suggested a walk in Vedado to find coffee to take home. We looked for a grocery store but weren't having any luck. I had yet to realize that people tend to shop daily, and most of their food is bought from specialized vendors or small *bodegas*. We came upon an outdoor vegetable market with a small grocery kiosk, and I spied some coffee on a shelf. We sidled up to the window and in my best Spanish I told the gentleman, *"Doce café, por favor,"* and he looked at me like I had just lost my mind. A lady standing near me knew what

I was up to. She made a gesture by kissing her fingers telling me the coffee is *bueno,* but I already knew that. Because Cubans never move too quickly, the transaction had taken some time, and there was now quite a queue behind us. When the clerk told me in Spanish how much I owed him, my mind went blank, and I was left standing there with an equally blank look on my face. Not to worry, all the people I had been holding up lent a helping hand and someone translated for me. I told myself, "I really must master Spanish."

After that accomplishment I was feeling quite pleased with myself and thought a Coppelia ice cream cone was in order. Jesús had pointed out the Coppelia ice cream location last year and I thought I could find it again. We searched for a few minutes, and Carene was beginning to get cranky. I knew she would rather a mojito over an ice cream cone any day, but I was on a mission. When I saw a friendly-looking female coming toward us, I thought I'd ask her. I didn't try to impress her with my Spanish, but instead used my best pantomime, making a motion like I was licking an ice cream cone. She looked at me with a straight face, and in perfect English asked if I was looking for Coppelia ice cream. That caused Carene and me to burst out laughing, which I'm sure made her think we were both loco. When we arrived and saw a long line-up we changed our minds. There is a separate line for tourists but there was no way I was going ahead of the locals who had been standing there forever. We went back to the hotel for mojitos instead.

For dinner, we decided to try a restaurant across from the hotel. It sits below sidewalk level, so you walk down some steps to enter. Because the nicer restaurants with air conditioning usually have it turned up so high, we find it uncomfortable, so we asked if we could sit at one of the tables outside. A young hostess followed us out with menus and we ordered drinks. We couldn't believe the array of choices offered so it took us quite some time to decide what to have. The hostess returned with our drinks then took her position, standing about five feet behind us. This was not only making the two of us uncomfortable, but we were also feeling sorry for her.

I was torn between rabbit or chicken, while Carene was deciding between pork and beef. We finally made our decisions then motioned to the hostess. I ordered rabbit and was told, "No rabbit today," so chose chicken stuffed with "fruits", not quite knowing what to expect. Carene opted for pork and was told, "No pork today", so she chose beef. We wondered why the waitress hadn't told us what wasn't available before we mulled over the menu. The meal was mediocre and we realized why we like eating in paladares. Because some ingredients are difficult to obtain in Cuba, the restaurants that try to get fancy just can't. My green beans were canned and my stuffed baked potato had seen better days. While we ate, the hostess remained standing behind us. We assumed she had been told to do so, in case we needed something, so we made a big production telling each other how wonderful everything was in hopes she would leave. It didn't work. When I finished my meal, she came to remove my plate and asked me if I would like dessert. I chose flan de huevos which arrived while Carene was still chewing away on her beef. They were trying so hard to be formal, but all we wanted was the waitress to stop standing at attention behind us.

We were joining the Muraleando group for a day of "camping" in Parque Lenin. Cubans refer to a day in a park, or just getting out of the city as camping.

*Parque Lenin, twelve miles south of central Havana, occupies an area of 1,840 acres and is a very popular destination for *Habaneros*. It was created in the 1970s as an amusement park for children and an area of greenery.

Jesús, his daughter, Jenny, and Carlos picked us up in the morning to take us to Muraleando where we would catch the bus to Parque Lenin. When we arrived, the bus was parked in front of Manolo's and a flurry of activity was taking place. Artists, family, and friends were milling about, while all kinds of things were being loaded into the storage compartment of the bus. There were boxes and bags, chairs, blankets, balls, guitars and even a pup tent. The bus, a new one imported from China, was highly decorated. There was large gold Christmas garland stretched across the top of the windshield with plastic flowers woven through, and small stuffed animals hanging down. An ever-present religious icon hung from the mirror. Because drivers usually drive the same bus at all times, they take great pride in it, treating it as if it was their own. There is always something to wipe your feet on as you enter the bus.

When it was time to leave, the music was turned on, loud and upbeat. We had a few stops to make and I was amazed how the driver manoeuvered the bus with such ease through the narrow streets of Muraleando. Our first stop was at the house where the newest mural had been painted. Some artists got off with the three Canadian girls we had met at the school so they could view it. Jesús had told us that the people who live in the house sometimes do cooking for parties in Muraleando. Manolo came out of the house carrying a big plastic bin holding something wrapped in the Cuban version of a red checkered cloth – mauve flowered curtain material. The bin was stowed in the storage compartment, everyone got back on the bus, and we were off again. We made three more stops, one for rum, one for bread and one for soda for the children. As we drove along, I watched as Manolo and Mayra were busy with business. While we were all footloose and fancy free, they were still working, and it gave me pause to think how dedicated to Muraleando they are.

At the park, we didn't drive in the main entrance, but instead pulled over to the side of the road where everyone got off. The first order of business was to take a group picture of us all standing beside the bus, and then the unloading began. Everyone was grabbing something to carry, but every time I tried it would be taken from me. Cuba is such a matriarchal society they won't allow women, especially ones like me that aren't spring chickens, to do anything. Everything was carried across a large grassy area to a spot beside a stream, under some trees. There was a lot of activity, and everyone seemed to know what needed to be done. People laid their bags down and some chairs were set up. Near the road there was a thatched roof cook shack with four dogs milling around, probably hoping to score some food later. Two men went to the cook shack and came back with three tables and benches for dominoes. The children were already running around playing with a ball, and a few of the young men kicked a soccer ball around. The grass was so dry it was like straw and, even though their feet were bare, I didn't see anyone flinch. As I stood marvelling at all of the activity, plastic glasses appeared and were passed out. Mayra produced a flask of her wonderful café and poured everyone about three fingers. Nothing officially begins in Cuba until you have café.

Three folding lawn chairs had been set up under the trees and, since there were three older people with us, I assumed the chairs were for them. When Jesús told me they had rented the chairs, and that one had been rented for me, did I ever feel old! I know Cubans constantly offer their seat to a guest, but they really didn't have to rent me a chair. Everyone else had blankets laid on the ground and the only other seats were the little benches at the domino tables. I found the whole chair thing quite funny but at the same time very sweet.

After café, out came the dominoes and the rum. Amid chatter, laughter and even friendly yelling, one game began while another was getting started a few feet away. I got up from my rented chair and wandered over to watch, but as soon as I did, one of the artists jumped up offering me his seat on the bench. I wondered how he was going to play dominoes standing up, and finally convinced him I didn't need his seat. I could see this was making him uncomfortable, so I relented and shared a bench with Carene. The bottle of rum sat on the ground against the table leg, along with a can of cola. They drink the rum with just a splash of cola and no ice. Mario had offered Carene some, and when she gave me a sip I found it tasted pretty good, with the cola just taking the edge off the rum. Here we were again, drinking rum before noon. I made a mental note that if we did this again, I would bring along a bottle of rum.

The bin we picked up in Muraleando with the mauve curtain material had me intrigued because, when I caught a whiff, something smelled wonderful. Later, Mayra removed the cloth and offered everyone a croquette. I inquired what they were and was told, *papa rellenas* or stuffed potatoes. I took a bite and found soft, warm mashed potatoes that had been formed into a ball, then rolled in bread crumbs and fried. In the centre was about a tablespoon of a ground meat mixture that had been cooked with spices and tomato. As Victor (the older one) explained, you never know what will be in the centre – it's a surprise. They were absolutely delicious, and one of the first things I did after returning home was find a recipe.

I had been told there were washrooms in the park and began to wonder where they were. I wasn't suffering, just wondering. A little later Grandma and her sister walked away from the group, disappearing into some trees. As I watched, I wondered if there was a washroom that I couldn't see, but knew it was just wishful thinking and bided my time.

Dominoes were still being played, with the losers giving up their seats to another team. Carene and I were watching and learning because our turn was coming up. The men banged their tiles down on the table with great enthusiasm, just like some men bang playing cards down in Canada. When our turn came, we made sure we banged our tiles down with great aplomb. My face was beginning to hurt from all the laughing and I kept thinking how much joy these people get out of life. It seemed that they never stopped smiling and laughing with each other. When Manolo and his partner beat us, they broke into a chorus of olé olé, olé olé, amid more laughter. I guess olé olé is a universal thing, as is the wave that was also being done around the table. Later, when Carene was playing another game, she was serenaded by two guitars and the maracas. I had no idea why, but everyone sure thought it was funny.

Mayra was still busy working and every so often I could see her discussing something with Manolo. Mario came and asked if Carene and I wanted to share a chicken for lunch or would we each like a whole one. I didn't ask questions, just told him we would share one.

Nature was now calling, so I asked Carene to walk with me to the phantom washrooms. With tissues in hand, we wandered along the same path that Grandma and her sister had taken. I gave it a go first while Carene stood guard and soon we had company. One of the little girls from the group thought she would join us and stood chatting with Carene while I took care of business. When it was Carene's turn the little girl stayed by her side. While Carene squatted, she told me a case of stage fright had come over her, since she wasn't prepared for company. The little girl made no move to leave until Carene was done, or I should say, not done. I'm not a good squatter at the best of times and wondered how Grandma and her sister had managed. My guess was practice makes perfect.

The activity continued and everyone was having a wonderful time. When two small horses and their handlers appeared, Jenny ran over to tell Jesús the exciting news, so in English, he told her to go and find out how much a ride would cost. Jesús was trying to teach Jenny English, but found when he asked her something in English, she wouldn't answer him. Not the case when it came to a horse ride though, she ran to the horses and promptly returned telling Jesús the price of a ride. For a few pesos the children could have a ride, or be walked by a handler around the field. Everyone who wanted one had a ride and even Mario took a couple of turns around the field.

Around two o'clock, a man from the cook shack made his way across the grass. He was wearing a straw hat, an apron and rubber boots, and on his shoulder he carried a tray piled high with gorgeous looking BBQ chickens. All the dogs that had been around the cook shack were trailing behind him, but at an appropriate distance. Another man carried a tray loaded with individual boxes containing rice, beans, salad and a chunk of squash. As everyone gathered around to admire the delicious looking lunch, a couple of men held up chickens while the cook stood between them for a photo-op.

The lunch was passed out and everyone dug in. I was having a little trouble as I wasn't used to the Cuban way of dining al fresco. There were no tables here and the only eating utensil was a small plastic fork. My cardboard box was getting limp on the bottom and I wasn't savvy on how to rip a chicken apart. I like to use a napkin throughout a meal, but of course there were none. If I could have just figured out how to get some of the scrumptious meat away from the carcass I would have been more successful. I ended up eating the wings and Carene ate a bit then we gave the rest of our chicken to Victor who was more than happy to receive it.

There were no garbage cans, but instead, a small area surrounded on three sides by a hand-made fence. As people finished eating, they threw their remains into this area. Now it was the dogs turn to eat and as one crunched down on a chicken bone I thought, they get so little meat, that they weren't going to let a chicken bone stand in their way.

After lunch Manolo climbed into the pup tent and some of the other men were lying here and there on the grass for siesta time. Things became quiet but not for long.

Some from the group were taking the children to the amusement area, so we joined them. There were about fifteen of us, and as we strolled along, I noticed how beautiful the florae in the park were, with the flowering trees in full bloom. Yosiet was walking with his little girl, holding her hand as she chattered away. I heard her say, "Papa?" and he answered softly, "Si?" then she chattered away some more. She was assuring him she wanted to go on some rides. When she was having a horse ride earlier, she had become frightened and began to cry, so Yosiet had to pretend he was a horse, and give her a ride on his shoulders instead.

Mario stayed pretty close to Carene and me as he likes to practise his English whenever he can. We talked about many things and he told us of his life's goals and his musical plans. When he said that one of his idols is Snoop Dogg, and I told him that Carene had met him, his eyes became the size of saucers and his jaw dropped. Carene said she and Snoop Dogg weren't pals, but she had only met him when he was a client in the spa where she worked. I don't think it mattered – he was still pretty impressed with her brush with stardom.

Tickets for the rides were bought and passed out. The artists were like big kids and as excited as the children. Carene and I were trying to convince them that with the heat, and having just eaten lunch, it was best if we passed on the rides. I'm afraid we were looking like Canadian wimps, but, we are Canadian wimps. They all piled onto different rides, laughing and waving at us. When Yosiet took his little girl on a kiddie ride of elephants, all we could hear was her wailing every time they passed us. They all got off the last ride and I noticed that Manolo wasn't looking well. His face had turned a shade of green and he moaned, telling us his *pollo* was sitting in a ball and going up and down inside him. I really thought he was going to lose his lunch and I was thankful we had passed on the rides, wimps or not.

Now it was time for ice cream. We went to a canteen with a covered area with tables and chairs. They didn't offer thirty-one flavours like Baskin Robbins, but they did offer chocolate. Ice cream was ordered and served in glass dishes with spoons. While we sat eating our ice cream, Manolo's colour began to return. When everyone was finished and the children needed cleaning up, they took a bottle of water, poured some over their hands and wiped their faces. No fuss, no muss.

An announcement told everyone it was five o'clock and the amusement area would be closing. As we walked back to the rest of the group, we saw workers walking toward the main gate to catch a bus home and a couple of men pushing a car to get it going, which is a common sight in Cuba.

Back with the rest of the group, we were all offered small croquettes, but I was offered one of the few papa rellenas that were left. I wasn't the least bit hungry, but couldn't turn down this new discovery. As I sat on my rented chair between the two grandmas, I looked around and felt like I was in heaven. Every so often Mayra's mother would smile and squeeze my hand and I would touch her soft face.

The guitars came out and it was time for a sing-along. I have participated in many sing-alongs, but this one was different. Instead of people trying to out-sing each other, usually off key, everyone sang softly, while two guitars were quietly strummed and people took turns on the maracas. I didn't know the words they were singing, but it all sounded lovely. There was the odd solo, and even a short, quiet rap by Mario. Nivia had brought along her little nephew, and as he sat on her lap, he was fading fast. Before long he was asleep, so they wrapped him in a blanket, laid him under a tree, and he was quite content. This was quiet time and all very peaceful. I had that now familiar mushy feeling in my stomach yet again.

Jesús had called the hotel asking for my full name, and what name Carene went by. In Cuba the use of last names is quite different than in

Canada. Last names carry both the paternal and maternal family names and are hyphenated. When a woman marries she doesn't take her husband's name, but keeps her family name. My name would be Bonnie Sinclair-Carroll, with Sinclair being my father's, and Carroll being my mother's family names. That would mean Carene's name would be Carene Martin-Sinclair. Because of that phone call I had the feeling something was planned for us today, but I certainly wasn't prepared for what was to come.

Nivia called everyone to gather around and Jesús positioned himself between Carene and me to translate. Manolo began speaking and it wasn't long before I crumbled. Through a haze I heard how much it means to them that we returned yet again, and they appreciate all we do for them. I was presented with The Key to Muraleando and told they don't give keys to just anyone, but that we are considered family. The key, a homemade one was forged from metal and mounted on a piece of stained wood. It was made to look like an old fashioned key and had MURALEANDO etched onto it. Next we were given paintings done by Manolo, and Carene was also given a handmade necklace and bracelet, made by one of the artists. By now I was a mess, and Nivia kept telling me in her heavily accented English, "Boonee, breathe!" After I took a few deep breaths and gained some composure there was more to come. Nivia had decorated and painted two bottles which she presented to us and they were beautiful. The artists were experimenting with different forms of material and I felt honoured that she had taken so much time with these.

Because I couldn't speak, Carene made a lovely acceptance speech for us both, telling them how much Cuba means to me, and that she was happy to be able to experience it with me. When I gained enough composure to say a few words, I thanked them for all their kindness, and told them how much I love them all, and how much I love Cuba. Many pictures were taken and there were lots of kisses and hugs all around.

When the bus arrived to take us home, everyone lent a hand with the clean-up. As the tables and benches were being returned to the cook shack, I tried to take a bench but it was promptly taken from me. Next I tried to take my rented chair back to the bus but that was also taken. I gave up and walked to the bus carrying my knapsack.

I thought we would all be getting off the bus at Manolo's but apparently different arrangements had been made. When we arrived back in Muraleando we made a stop and Nivia and her gang got off. Because I was clued out as to what was happening, I only realized that this was good-bye when she started blowing us kisses. I felt bad because I hadn't given her a proper good-bye, but realized it was probably better this way. I'm never good at saying good-bye, and with my emotions running high it wouldn't have been a pretty sight.

We made a few more stops with people getting off here and there. There were different levels of good-byes, ranging from quick waves to hugs and kisses. At Manolo's, Mario asked the driver to wait so he could run home to get one of his CD's. He took the time to write a personal message on it then presented it to us. The driver waited patiently, all the while smiling.

Jesús spoke to the bus driver, and then told me if I gave the driver 6 CUC, he would drop us very close to the Hotel Nacional. All that were left on the bus with us were Jesús and Jenny, the two Victors and an artist I'll call the Rasta. The bus stopped and everyone got up to leave. Jesús gave Carene and me big hugs and kisses and promises were made to see each other for Muraleando 2010. I was in the aisle seat, and because we were both standing, we had to lean out for hugs. Next up the aisle was Victor (the tall one), who was laughing his familiar laugh, telling us how jealous his girlfriend would be if she saw him hugging us. Victor (the older one) hugged us good-bye and behind him was the Rasta. This trip was the first time I had seen him and his look intrigued me. He had short dreads and always wore a bandana. He had big blood-shot eyes and usually had the stub of a large cigar in his mouth. Remember, they aren't big on introductions in Cuba, so I never did learn his name. That morning when he and I had come face to face on the street, I pushed my shyness aside and greeted him the Cuban way, with a kiss. When he reached us, I hugged him and received a good strong hug back. I sat down so Carene could reach over to hug him, and as she did I heard a tiny yelp come from her. He smiled a mischievous smile then got off the bus. When she sat back down I asked her, "Did you get a major hug from the Rasta?" Her reply came back, "YES! My cheek is bruised, my ribs are cracked, and I think we might be engaged."

It was just us on the bus now and we laughed about our huge taxi. When the bus driver let us off, we did get the odd stare from people on the street, but we just waved as he pulled away like it was an ordinary occurrence.

Both of us were drained, happy, hungry, and thirsty all at the same time, so after quick showers we headed down to the hotel BBQ. The restaurant was busy and our favourite house band was playing. How perfect for our last night. We ordered mojitos and, scanning the menu, I saw that they were offering ropa vieja. I love the dish but so far on this trip I hadn't had it.

The meal was delicious as were the mojitos. The band was fabulous and te surroundings optimal. I was so high on life, I was in the clouds, and there it was again, that warm mushy feeling in my stomach.

Observations and Reflections - 2009

Again this year, my first reflection will be on Fidel Castro. As a person who believes in angels, I think Fidel has been blessed with an abundance of them surrounding him throughout his life. He has survived numerous assassination attempts, time in prison and torture. As I continue to learn about Cuba through visiting and reading, my opinion of him has pretty much stayed the same. I realize he has his faults, but on the whole, he has done wonders for the people of Cuba, and most of them love him dearly. I have a great deal of respect for the man.

There are all colours of skin in Cuba, but their philosophy is, we're all Cuban. It is a matriarchal society, so motherhood is held in high esteem. Pregnant women receive special treatment, ranging from medical care to housing. Women are treated as equals, and Cubans adore their children, also treating them with respect. It seems there is a lot of respect going around in Cuba.

In richer countries where everyone is trying to get ahead, it's easy to forget about your fellow man. In Cuba, they help each other and generally have each other's backs. Greed somehow disappears when everyone is pretty much in the same boat.

The people of Cuba have always struggled, but one of the worst times for them was during the Special Period. Because it has been a relatively short time since then, people remember it vividly. Like people who lived through the Great Depression, they don't forget hard times, and they never take anything for granted.

Cuba has its own "Café Society", perhaps stemming from Spanish influences. Café is a very social thing. When you visit someone's home the first thing you are offered is a seat and the second is café.

They're not big on formal introductions in Cuba. If you are a friend of my friend, then you are a friend of mine.

Even though Cuba is a poor country, the people still like to own pets and treat them well. Their animals basically eat food scraps, and not much meat, but are still well cared for.

Garbage continues to be a problem in Cuba but they certainly do reduce, reuse and recycle. Cubans have been using reusable bags for a long time and usually carry one with them at all times. They still use more paper products than plastic.

Section Four

April 2010

Bonnie Martin

Bonnie and Dr. Rodovaldo, Las Terrazas – 2010

Benito, a tobacco farmer in Vinales – 2010

People You'll Meet

Adelaida Garcia - Casa #42, 21 & O

Adelaida is an artist and the owner of a casa located in a building at the intersection of *Calle* 21 & *Calle* O. The building is referred to as 21 & O. I was made to feel very welcome at her casa and have stayed with her many times.

Lincoln - Casa Teresita - Casa #54, 21 & O

This casa is owned by Lincoln and his wife. They are lovely people and their apartment is absolutely beautiful.

Purry

Purry is the owner of a casa in Viñales. Her home is very comfortable with a beautiful outdoor dining area.

Dr. Rodovaldo - Medical doctor in Las Terrazas

Dr. Rodovaldo treated me when I became ill in 2010. He gave me excellent care and I now consider him a friend.

Barbara - Juan's host in Las Terrazas

Barbara runs one of the community houses, Villa Ciriles, in Las Terrazas. She lives with her husband, Cirilo, and their daughter, Rye.

Chapter Seven

In 2010 there would be some changes in Carene's and my Cuban adventures. Previously, our trips had been in mid-April, but this year we planned to visit a little later to enable us to experience May Day in Cuba. By stretching our holiday into eleven days, we could take two side trips – one to Viñales and one to Las Terrazas.

Because our time in Havana would be split, we would only stay at the Hotel Nacional for three nights, and then move across the road to a casa particular. Jesús had been recommending casas to us, telling us they would be a good alternative to hotels.

On arrival day we checked in and, in keeping with tradition, went out back to the rock, ordered our first mojitos, and toasted being in Cuba. Sitting at the edge of the rock, looking over the water, we basked in the beautiful temperatures and felt very fortunate to be here again.

We had arrangements to meet Jesús our first morning to conduct some business, and then do some touring. He had booked the hotel in Las Terrazas through a travel agency. We would go to the agency, pay for our rooms, and receive vouchers to present upon check-in. This system makes check-in at the hotel much easier.

With our business taken care of, our plan for the day was to take the ferry to Casablanca. We took a city bus to the ferry, which was a first for us in Cuba. In 2007 Cuba purchased new buses from China, so I had changed my mind about not taking public transport. There was no way I would ride on one of the old camel buses, but the new ones were a big improvement.

When we arrived at the ferry, I was curious as to why our purses and bags were checked, and we were scanned with a metal detector. When I questioned Jesús he relayed a story telling me why.

Ferry Hijacking - April 2003

On April 2, 2003, the ferry that travels between Havana and Regla was hijacked by eight men, who were armed with knives and a gun. There were fifty people on board, including some children and tourists. The hijackers wanted to take the ferry to the USA but, not far into international waters, the boat ran out of fuel. The Cuban authorities, with a promise of fuel, persuaded the hijackers to allow the ferry to be towed to Mariel. The hijackers had threatened female passengers at knife point, telling them they would throw them overboard if the ferry was not refuelled. Upon arrival at Mariel, one woman jumped overboard out of fear. When that occurred, some men on board took the opportunity to wrestle with the hijackers. Cuban security forces had divers waiting underwater who commandeered the boat and rescued the hostages without firing a shot.

Justice is swift in Cuba. Because there were weapons involved, and children and tourists aboard, the hijackers were dealt with sternly. After a trial, three of the men were executed, on April 11, 2003, and five received life sentences.

Casablanca is just across the bay from Havana, so the ferry ride takes about seven minutes. When we arrived, we went to an outdoor café for a cold drink and, with the harbour on one side, and the village on the other, it was very pleasant. When Jesús and Maria married, they held their wedding reception in the same café.

After leaving the café, we went to the Hersey train stop. The Hersey train is the oldest electrical train in Cuba, and it begins in Casablanca, travelling east to Matanza Province every day. Matanza Province has many beautiful beaches and is the location of the resort area of Varadero. Jesús was excitedly checking the train schedule, saying he could take the train to the beach, spend the day, and be home by about four p.m. Because most Cubans don't own cars, they find any way they can to have time away from the city.

We walked to the small town square that had a church, but not much else. A young boy was playing with an old tire, rolling, and then chasing it. The heat didn't seem to be bothering him, but I was tired just watching. When we caught up to him, I asked if I could take his picture. He agreed and posed beside his tire with a big smile.

We began to climb a long set of stairs that would lead us to the top of the hill and the statue of Cristo de la Habana. Because of the heat, Jesús warned us to take our time. Off to one side of the stairs were small homes with manicured gardens. Some had signs offering food for sale, and it was explained Cubans will find many ways to try and make ends meet. A man sat watching his goat and her kids graze, and I thought what a peaceful and beautiful place to call home. About half way up the stairs Jesús suggested we sit on the steps for a rest. We sat on the steps, looking at the harbour in the distance, and began to chat. I asked Jesús a little about his life and he began telling us his story.

Jesús

When Jesús was twelve years old he wanted to be an artillerist. He attended a military school, named after the Cuban hero, Camilo Cienfuegos. The students were referred to as *camilitos*, which means small Camilos. He studied there for four years, until the age of sixteen, learning how to shoot Russian 85 mm cannons against tanks and boats. He was then selected to study at a language faculty in Russia for one year, to become a professor of Russian language for the armed forces of Cuba.

In 1974, at the age of eighteen, he travelled back to Russia for four years, only returning to Cuba once, making the trip by boat. He returned from Russia in 1978 and, for the next three years, did social service as a military translator, teaching Russian to Cuban colonels and generals. From then, he worked at the Science Academy as a simultaneous interpreter of Russian, and as an expert in scientific co-operation until 1994. During that time he visited the Soviet Union twenty times, as well as other socialist countries in Europe, China, and Mongolia.

He was married from 1986 until 1992. With Jesús travelling so much during the Special Period, his wife became unhappy. She wanted to move to Miami which she finally did, ending the marriage.

Later, he did various things to eke out a living. One was selling small perfumes, bought from a middleman in Havana. He used to travel about twenty kilometres by bicycle to his sister's home, leaving perfume with her to sell. The following week he went back to collect the money and leave more perfume. He also sold shoes, T-shirts and other items, with the help of a diplomat from the Nicaraguan embassy, who he met when they were both studying English. Jesús felt knowing English would make it easier for him to earn a living.

In 1997 Jesús met Maria. They were married in 2003, and are very happy.

Jesús had come to know Miguel, one of the artists from Muraleando. Miguel called Jesús inviting him to Muraleando to see a project he had helped start there. Jesús said as soon as he saw it he knew he had to become involved.

Carene commented to me later how much she had enjoyed our chat with Jesús. It is hard to get him to sit and relax for long because he wants to give his clients a full day for their money. Sitting on the steps and learning about his life was a nice change.

*Casablanca is best known for the Cristo de la Habana, a sixty-foot tall white marble statue of Christ, which looms over the village. The statue was commissioned by President Batista's wife, Marta. She had made a vow that she would finance a large statue of Christ if her husband survived the attack by students on the presidential palace in 1957. The statue was completed a week prior to the Revolution. It can be seen from many parts of the city, and is familiar to all Cubans.

Near the statue, Jesús pointed out a park with concession booths, as well as the Che museum, now all sitting unused. He said families used to be able to get out of the city easily, spending time in the park, picnicking, and playing baseball. After the ferry hijacking in 2003, the state discouraged visits to Casablanca. It seemed to me to be a case of "throwing the baby out with the bath water".

After returning from Casablanca, we had lunch at a paladar and then continued sight-seeing around Havana. Near the train station, Jesús shouted to a woman on the second floor of a tenement, who turned out to be his sister-in-law, Maria's sister. We crossed the street, so I assumed we were going to pay her a visit. I remembered that in Cuba you are always welcome into someone's home. The familiar saying, "my casa is your casa" came to mind.

A Moment in Time - Visiting a humble home in Havana

We entered a building, climbed some very narrow stairs, and made our way down an equally narrow hallway. There was some writing on the wall, and as Jesús read it, he began to chuckle. It had been written by his sister-in-law and it read, "I rise very early in the morning so I'd better not catch you peeing here." My guess was that in some of the buildings, derelict people enter and sleep in the hallways.

We knocked on the door and were welcomed into a very humble home. It consisted of two small rooms, one being the kitchen, and one the living room. Off the living room a small balcony was strung with clotheslines, and the lady of the house was hanging clothes she had just laundered by hand. Laundry is a daily chore in Cuba and it is a common sight to see clothes hanging on balconies. A little girl about three years of age sat on the floor playing with a few green plastic houses from a Monopoly game. The only furnishings were two old folding chairs, a small TV with rabbit ears, and an old dilapidated ghetto blaster. Behind the first room, a kitchen held a sink and a hot plate, but no refrigerator. From the kitchen a set of crudely made wooden stairs led to a loft where the family slept on mattresses. I thought my heart would break. We in Canada have so much, while these people have so little.

We were introduced to Daniel, Jesús' nephew. He is an acrobat and works with a partner performing at various events. Someone from

Russia had seen them perform and invited them to go to Russia to train with the Russian circus. They were to leave in August, and would be in Russia for two years. This was a wonderful opportunity which Jesús and Maria had a lot to do with. When Daniel's mother had to leave Havana and move to the country for health reasons, Jesús and Maria had Daniel live with them, knowing it would be better for his future.

We took some pictures with the family and wished Daniel luck in his new venture. When we were leaving I saw Jesús do his thing, discreetly passing his sister-in-law some money. It was just another example of Jesús' strong family ties.

We had arranged to have Jesús take us to see the casa at 21 & O where we would move on Friday. It is a beautiful art deco apartment building with casas throughout, owned and run by different people. It was constructed in 1943 by a businessman who had an office on the first floor and an apartment on another floor. When you enter, you walk down a short entranceway to a circular lobby with apartments organized around the circle. The lobby forms an atrium that rises through the entire five storeys of the building. A skylight decorated with a sun/moon image is located directly above a large statue that sits in the centre of the lobby. A circular marble staircase winds along the outer edge of the atrium and continues to the top floor.

When reading about casas, I learned that some offer multiple rooms, and because I had requested two rooms, I assumed we would be staying in one with them. As it turned out, we would be in two different casas, on different floors. I was a little thrown by this arrangement, and wished we had stayed at the Hotel Nacional. Nevertheless, we made arrangements with two different casas, telling them we would check in on Friday morning for three nights.

I wanted to take in some music this trip, so Juan arranged for us to attend an informal jam session where some troubadours from The Isle of Youth would be performing. I didn't realize it at the time, but the jam was held on one side of the Egrem studio, which is where the Buena Vista Social Club CD had been recorded in 1998. Juan was waiting for us when we arrived, and things were in full swing. The audience, mainly young people, were partying like mad, while they shared bottles of rum. Musicians were playing on a stage, and every so often someone from the audience would be called up to perform. Jesús told us the troubadours travelled at their own expense to perform for the sheer joy of it, and their love of music. I came to the conclusion that musicians are the same the world over – they love hanging out with other musicians, and love to jam and party. This group was no different.

It was early evening when we left the jam, and Jesús wanted to treat us to Coppelia ice cream. I had heard so much about this ice cream that people wait in line for, and now I was going to finally experience it. You have to remember, Cuban people are very patient, and used to standing in queues for many things, so standing in line for ice cream is no big deal. For them it is a good excuse to visit.

Today we would visit Muraleando which is always a highlight of my trips to Cuba. First, we went to the bus station to purchase our tickets for Viñales and Las Terrazas. Just like the experience at the travel agent, purchasing our bus tickets would be a very different process for me. We went into a separate room and Jesús told a woman behind a desk what we wanted. We showed our passports, and Jesús showed Juan's Cuban ID card, then the agent wrote out the tickets. It seemed they have a system for everything in Cuba, and it all works well. With our business completed, we now had to find transportation to take us to Muraleando. We weren't having much luck, but Jesús isn't one to give up easily. He approached a man with a very odd-looking vehicle, who agreed to take us. It was an old Second World War motorcycle, with an attached covered trailer that held bench seats down each side. When we pulled up to a corner in Muraleando where some artists were working, they didn't bat an eye as we climbed down from our ride. I could now add this vehicle to my ever-growing list of modes of transportation I experienced while in Cuba.

Every year, the artists of Muraleando complete a special project, and this year's was a large one. On a street from one barrio to another, they had painted murals and erected some sculptures, naming the project The Boulevard of Friendship.

Muraleando was hosting an art exhibition at The Club. They were expecting five buses, with people from Turkey and Greece. We had seen some Mercedes-Benz cars, flying Turkish flags, lined up in the driveway of the Hotel Nacional, as well as a large police presence, leading us to believe the guests were people of importance. The Club had been readied and everyone's art was on display. A bartender had been hired, and Irasema, the salsa dancer from Muraleando, and her son Kevin were going to dance. The plan was for the guests to walk The Boulevard of Friendship, and then go to The Club to view the art and socialize.

Because I had brought gifts for everyone, we made our way to Manolo's before the art exhibition began. Everyone was busy getting ready for the big event, and I was feeling very intrusive. Manolo was in and out, and Mayra kept coming out of the kitchen, both of them apologizing for not spending time with us. We visited in the living room while people popped in to see us, taking time out of their busy day.

Among the gifts, I had brought a pair of Celtic knot earrings for Mayra's mother Erminda, who holds a special place in my heart. When I presented them to her, Jesús explained that a Celtic knot intertwines and never ends (like our friendship). She became very emotional and began to cry, telling me they meant a great deal to her.

Mayra fed the artists, and when they had finished, Manolo, Jesús, Carene and I sat down to one of Mayra's wonderful meals. We had rice, mixed with ham, eggs and black beans, somewhat like Chinese fried rice. There was fruit, homemade pineapple juice and Cuban salad. Dessert was *orange de toronja*, a marmalade type jelly, served with grated cheese on top.

I am always touched by the planning that I know goes into our visits. It doesn't matter what is going on in Muraleando, they still go out of their way for us. I gave Manolo a donation for the cause, and as always, he was very grateful. During lunch Manolo invited us to attend a pig roast, being held the next day in Parque Lenin, for the wind-up of Muraleando 2010. We told him we would be honoured.

As the time neared for the expo to begin, the grey overcast skies were making me nervous. Unfortunately, just before the guests were to arrive, it started to pour rain. This turn of events seemed to upset Carene and me more than the artists. In a country where they are used to many obstacles, they didn't let this one bother them, but instead came up with an alternate plan. The art was moved under shelter and they arranged for the buses to pull up to the entrance of The Club one at a time, and then the people would get off the bus and view the art. Because sheltered space was limited, I'm sure sales were affected. Even though the people had been told in a speech at the beginning of the expo that proceeds from the sales would all go to help Muraleando's work in the community, I was dismayed when I watched as people bartered, but the artists took it all in stride and never stopped smiling.

We checked out of the Hotel Nacional and moved to the casas at 21 & O, dropped our bags, and then made our way to Muraleando to catch the chartered bus to Parque Lenin.

People began to arrive and most of the artists had family with them. The plan for the day was a baseball game between the men, some music and of course, the pig roast. We went to a different area of the park from where we had been last year, and I was pleased to see a small pavilion with washroom facilities. A friendly dog wandered around, and like most dogs in Cuba, he had a unique personality.

The men divided themselves into two teams and the baseball game got underway. There was a lot of laughter and a lot of rum involved in the game, but it was so hot, I was happy to just watch.

A Moment in Time – The arrival of the guest of honour

With the festivities in full swing, a small truck backed up to our area, and I could sense excitement in the air. It seemed the pig had arrived! He was displayed on a large slab and looked splendid, complete with a small straw hat and a cigar in his mouth. A photo op followed, and many group pictures were taken with the guest of honour.

The carving began, and the first thing to come off was the crackling. It was cut into small pieces and served from large banana leaves as an appetizer. I told myself I'd just have a small piece, after all, it's pure fat, but it was just so good I couldn't resist having more. Along with the pig there was a huge mound of *morro*, sweet potatoes and salad. Morro is rice and black beans cooked together, along with peppers, onions, garlic and cumin.

Some officials, as well as a professional singer, arrived, after which were some speeches. Manolo thanked everyone for all their hard work, and presented gift bags to those that aren't artists, but help out in other ways. Carene and I were also given some gifts, which we certainly weren't expecting.

The food still hadn't been served, but the thing is, with the heat in Cuba, you don't have to worry about food going cold. After the speeches, it was time to eat and everyone dug in. When everyone had eaten their fill, Manolo announced that the remaining pork could be divided up and taken home.

The singer performed, and later there was some dancing to taped music. It was around this time that we ran out of water, soda and beer. Between the dancing and the heat, I'm afraid I did a number on my body. Carene said she knew I was in trouble when, after I managed to find a can of beer, I guzzled it and announced to her, "I love beer! I'm going to drink it all the time!" It was all downhill from there.

I don't think I have ever been so thirsty, so when I saw we were packing up to leave, I was very happy. The bus ride back to Manolo's was long and quiet. I saw Jesús speaking to the bus driver, and assumed he was asking him if he would give us a ride to our casas. When I saw the driver shake his head no, I wanted to cry. There were a few people wanting rides from Manolo, and I knew we would be the last to be taken. We were given some water, which helped with my thirst, but I knew something wasn't right with me.

It was still dark out when I began hearing announcements coming from Revolution Square where May Day celebrations were being held. The reason we had come to Cuba at this time was to attend the celebration. We had arrangements to meet Juan and Jesús to go to the march, but because I wasn't feeling right, the thought of standing in Revolution Square, in the hot sun in a crowd of people wasn't appealing to me at all. Somehow I knew I shouldn't even try.

Carene was staying at Albertina's casa, and I joined her there for breakfast. I tried to eat, but had absolutely no appetite. I lay down on Carene's bed and asked her to apologize to Albertina for me. Carene went out to meet Jesús and Juan to explain that I wasn't well, and we wouldn't be going to the march. When she came back, she told me it was brutally hot out, and I would never have lasted. Because my hosts were attending the march, I couldn't get into my casa, so I went back to Albertina's and passed out on Carene's bed. She managed to get me up later to go to the Hotel Nacional for some soup. Right after, I went back to my casa and slept the rest of the day and through the night. I was feeling very guilty about leaving Carene on her own for the day, and wished we had stayed at the Hotel Nacional so she could have at least gone and sat by the pool. Needless to say, May Day was a total bust for me.

May second was my fortieth wedding anniversary and, because I was in Cuba, I found myself to be emotional. There was a mix up with my casa, and Albertina had been asked by my host to tell me I had to move. It was all very confusing, but in the end it worked out for the better. My new host, Adelaida, turned out to be a very nice woman and I have stayed with her many times since. I told Jesús to take my original hosts off his list of casas to recommend to clients.

After a fairly quiet day we were visiting the Lazaros and then were taking them out for dinner. They had done a lot of work to their home, getting it ready for Melina's upcoming fifteenth birthday celebration in August. They now had solid walls, painted in a cheery shade of turquoise, and the floors that were cement, were now covered with ceramic tiles.

Carene and I had brought some special gifts for Melina so we wanted to give them to her before dinner. The first gift was a bracelet with Friends Forever engraved on it. That is what we had named our group back in 2006, a name Melina had come up with. Carene gave Melina a dress she had worn at her high school prom as a gift. We thought it would fit her perfectly, and she could wear it at her party.

When Cuban people receive a gift they handle it differently than we do. They usually don't always open the gift, but if they do, they thank you politely, but don't really react much. If you give a gift to a child, they will take it to another room to open. This custom was difficult for me to get used to. I love giving gifts, and want the recipient to be as excited about receiving it as I am about giving it.

Melina opened the dress, smiled, said thank you, and left it sitting folded on her lap. She did approach us later, and through Juan told us she had dreamed of one day owning a dress as beautiful as the one we had given her. My final gift was a card with a Celtic tree of life depicted on the front, and I had Juan explain the meaning. I had put 150 CUC into the card, and Melina couldn't contain herself when she opened it. She let out a yelp which told me that it meant a great deal to her. I thought the money might help to pay for her party, or could be put away for her.

After the gift giving, we all walked to a paladar for dinner, and then later went to a café for some drinks and more visiting. I sat beside the father, and with Juan translating, we had a great conversation about Cuba. He had been brought up in a revolutionary home, so we talked a lot about politics. He was so into the conversation that Mom had to keep reminding him to slow down to allow Juan to translate. Carene told me later that when Melina and big brother's girlfriend had become a little bored with all the political talk, they began chatting and giggling with each other. Dad scolded them, telling them they should listen so they might learn something. It was a lovely evening but the time came to say our good-byes until another year. There were hugs and kisses all around and we wished Melina a good party.

Chapter Eight

Today we were travelling to Viñales and would stay at Purry's casa. Juan had taken us there last year for café, and it was then that I decided I wanted to return to this charming town. Because Viñales is a preserved colonial settlement, there are no hotels in the town. There is one about a quarter mile away, but most people who visit stay in one of the many casas.

Upon arrival, we were met with an odd sight. Standing on the sidewalk outside the small bus depot were about thirty people, all holding up signs advertising their casas. When we got off the bus, we were in the midst of a group of aggressive people, making it quite a challenge to retrieve our luggage.

Because it was so hot, and I wasn't feeling up to par, I told Juan I wanted to take it easy, so after lunch and walking around a little, we went back to Purry's to sit on her front arcade and watch the sights. When I couldn't stop yawning, Carene suggested that I go and lie down. I didn't feel ill, just extremely exhausted. I slept until early evening, and when they woke me for dinner, I had no appetite. I went back to bed and slept through the night.

Viñales is located in the province of Pinar del Río, where some of Cuba's finest tobacco is grown. We were going to visit a local tobacco farm, located at the end of the main street in town. We walked down a long driveway, past the storehouse, where there were two small houses, both painted white with bright blue trim, a common colour combination in Cuba. We were met by Benito, the farmer, who invited us into the storehouse where tobacco leaves hung on wooden beams in various stages of drying. He explained the drying process, then sat on a wooden chair, and with a board on his lap, demonstrated how cigars are rolled. He offered us a cigar, which we declined, but he lit up. Outside, he proudly pointed out his property lines and the family's vegetable gardens and then invited us into the house for café. On the kitchen table, a flask containing café sat with small demitasse cups beside. Benito's wife, a small woman, poured the café inviting us to sit in one of the many rocking chairs in the room. They don't charge a fee for their tours, but on the table there was a small dish to receive money. Benito chatted away, telling us he was sixty-nine years of age and a Baptist. He pulled a card out of his shirt pocket with a picture of John the Baptist, telling us he carries it at all times. As his wife looked on smiling, he told us she was of the Catholic faith. He went on to say he doesn't drink liquor, but smokes about twenty cigars a day, although he doesn't inhale. We were given a tour of their simple home which has been in the family for five generations. It contained very little furniture, but in the living room a piano sat regally. When I inquired if someone played, they said the piano used to belong to a sister, now deceased. There were many pictures of her on the piano, making me think it was a shrine to her memory.

We made our way back to Purry's to await our two p.m. bus that would take us to Las Terrazas.

Some History of Las Terrazas

The area, now known as Las Terrazas, began with coffee. After escaping the 1791 slave revolution in Haiti, French coffee growers established plantations in the hills around the area. Over time, Spaniards moved in, resulting in feelings of jealousy from the Spanish against the French settlers, until the French departed.

At one time there were approximately fifteen coffee plantations in the area. The land was ruined when the Spanish began overusing pesticides, resulting in poor quality coffee. For that reason, they couldn't get a good price for their coffee and merchants began importing cheaper coffee from Brazil.

At that time there wasn't a community in the area, just a few inhabitants living in the hills, cutting wood and making charcoal. They lived in temporary *ranchos*, and when the wood they were cutting became depleted, they would disassemble their homes and move. Because they were so isolated, it was difficult for them to purchase food or cloth, and equally difficult to sell their wood, charcoal or small animals. They had to use middlemen, resulting in their making very little money. To obtain emergency medical assistance, the people had to travel great distances over difficult terrain, either by mules or on foot. Sick or wounded people were moved in wheelbarrows made by hand.

Through time, life continued to be a struggle. People from other provinces or foreign people moved to the area, clear-cutting the trees, leaving the soil weak and then moving on repeating the process.

Exploitation continued when new, so-called owners showed up. With government backing, they introduced themselves as relatives of the Spaniards, telling the farmers that they had inherited the land. The original inhabitants were forced to buy what had once belonged to them, mortgaging what they purchased, amassing debts they couldn't pay. Parents and sons ended up being labourers of the new masters. This feudal system resulted in the accelerated devastation of the natural resources. The new owners didn't want to stay permanently, but just to prosper economically, using the profits to invest in other kinds of business.

The Revolution changed everything for the original people from the area. In January 1960 Fidel Castro gave land to thirty-six farmers who were descendants of the original inhabitants. The farm families and the charcoal burners interchanged their experiences, resulting in the transformation of the area by men who had the will to work and learn new jobs in a safe environment, unknown until then. The construction of the first part of Las Terrazas concluded in February 1971. The name, Las Terrazas, was born from an agreement of the neighbours who helped terrace the land and reforest it, with possibilities of expansion and other work. The foundation of Las Terrazas didn't become fulfilled quickly or easily, but there was a plan for a kind of socialist paradise that could be reached with the efforts of everybody.

They began building houses for the people. Originally there were twenty houses and today there are forty-five. At this writing, the population of Las Terrazas is 1,004.

The idea of building a hotel in Las Terrazas began in the seventies, but it wasn't until some years later that the project came to fruition. The nineties brought a radical change in the region. Moved by the need to find a solution to the new economic crisis, a new tourist project was born. To achieve this goal the creation of an infrastructure of hotel and gastronomic services was needed.

On September 12, 1991, the site where Hotel Moka would be built was chosen. On October 29 of the same year the first land removal began. During 1992 the biggest phase of the construction began, and finally on September 28, 1994, Moka hotel was inaugurated. The name of the hotel was taken from one of the coffee plantations the area at the beginning of the nineteenth century.

The aim was to have the community involved in the project, so the first guests in the hotel were the inhabitants of Las Terrazas. Today, the community is still involved in every aspect of the project. Every person employed in anything to do with the project is a member of the community.

Important personalities have visited this charismatic facility. In 1995 the people had the privilege of welcoming their Commander-in-Chief, Fidel Castro Ruz to the hotel, on February 14 and again on July 20.

Las Terrazas is a hidden gem that can be found a mere forty-five minutes west of Havana. Off the main highway, about five miles down the road, buses make a rest stop on the route from Havana to Pinar del Río and Viñales, giving people on the bus a glimpse of Las Terrazas. At this location there is a small lake, Lago El Palmar, a picnic area, and washrooms. People can purchase food and drinks at a small canteen, Rancho Curujey. Just across the way are the official offices for Las Terrazas. The village, along with Hotel Moka, is a short distance away.

Hotel Moka, a charming twenty-six room hotel, is situated atop one of the many terraced hills that surround the area. An open-air lobby has been built around a big tree, and off the lobby are a dining room, a small bar and a tuck shop.

As we were checking in, the girl at the desk told Juan she would fix him up with a good room in community housing. Community housing is a double room, like the ones in the hotel, added to one end of a house. The owner of the house is paid a monthly sum to look after the room and any guests. There are three houses offering community housing, but the inhabitants are trying to get the okay for more.

We went to our room and were thrilled with what we found. The bathroom area was especially unique. Off the main room was a dressing area and vanity, and beside that, shuttered doors leading to a toilet, bidet, and a bathtub with a shower. Beside the bathtub were floor to ceiling windows looking out to the trees beyond, allowing you to shower or bathe while viewing the foliage. The hotel is built in such a way that no one can see in the windows.

Not long after getting settled, there was a knock at our door and it was Juan, excited to the max, telling us, "This is crazy, sop (soap) and everything, just for me, this is crazy!" His excitement was funny to watch, and I came to the conclusion that he had probably never been in a hotel as nice as this one before.

When we were checking in, we learned of some tours and excursions that could be booked through the hotel so we booked a tour for the next day.

*Estacion Ecologica

This area of unspoilt Cuba has been declared a biosphere reserve by UNESCO. Woods consisting of tropical and deciduous trees and plants cover the Sierra del Rosario range, which is crossed by the Río San Juan with its small falls. The area is home to abundant, varied fauna: ninety species of birds as well as many different reptiles and amphibians. The walks here are lovely, on paths lined with flowers, including wild orchids.

We decided to take a walk and explore. From the hotel, and down many steps, we came upon Café Maria, a small café that sits about half way down one of the terraced hills. The café is open-air, and contains a small bar with stools, and about five tables. Historic pictures of plantations that once were close by adorn the walls. They offer many types of coffee, served the Cuban way in demitasse cups. It is a lovely place to sit and look over the surrounding beauty over delicious café.

Juan was anxious for us to see his room and meet his hosts, so down some steps we went, crossed a bridge, and then climbed more steps to his house. We were welcomed, and I could see why he was so thrilled. His room was spotlessly clean, and also had a unique bathroom. It contained the usual fixtures, but also had a separate enclosed outdoor shower that was lush with tropical plants. The floor of the shower was glass blocks, lit from below, and it was open on the top, allowing you to shower under the stars. We were offered café, but declined, telling Barbara we had just had some, so she told us to please come back the next day.

We climbed some more steps, and at the top of the hill was the town square, or what they call *La Plaza*, around which there was everything to accommodate the needs of the people.

Las Terrazas has two restaurants, attached to homes, and run by the families who live there. One, Fonda de Mercedes, serves traditional Cuban fare, and the other, El Romero, is a vegetarian restaurant.

We walked down a road dotted with houses and ended up at Casa de Botes, a boat house beside the Lago del San Juan, a small lake fed by the Río San Juan. It contained a few tables, and drinks, snacks, or light meals can be purchased there. It was beginning to get dark so we made our way back to the hotel dining room for dinner. During dinner I began feeling off again, so decided to have an early night, leaving Carene and Juan to do their thing

I had a bad night with chills and cramps, and knew I wasn't going to be able to partake in the tour to Estacion Ecologica, so Carene went and cancelled. She and Juan went for breakfast and I went back to bed. All I wanted to do was sleep. I vaguely remembered Carene coming back to the room to tell me that she and Juan were going to the river. I slept for hours, then through a fog, heard water dripping from somewhere in the bathroom. I went to investigate and found water all over the floor, dripping from the ceiling. I was so weak I could barely stand, but managed to go to the desk and told them the problem. I added that I needed to see the doctor. The woman told me I could change rooms, but I knew I couldn't do it by myself, so told her I would wait until Carene and Juan got back from the river. I slept some more but after a couple of hours decided to move. I threw our things into the suitcases, and with help from the bell man, moved upstairs to another room, and went back to bed. Later there was a knock at the door, and when I opened it, found Carene and Juan looking very worried. I explained everything and then told them I needed to eat something. We went to Fonda de Mercedes and I ordered chicken soup. Much to my dismay, they make everything from scratch, and although the soup was delicious, it took over an hour to arrive. While we waited, Carene and Juan had a tale to tell me.

A Moment in Time - Carene and Juan's adventure to the river

The sign on the road said, Río San Juan, with an arrow pointing the direction, so off they went, walking. What the sign didn't say was how far it was. They walked and walked in the heat, and even caught a ride part way. The man who gave them the ride assured them the river was close before he dropped them off. They walked farther, but between the unbearable heat and with Carene's water running out, and no river in sight, they decided to turn around. Carene said she had never been so hot in her life, and that she actually had salt stains on her sweat-soaked T-shirt.

While waiting for my soup, we heard someone calling to us. It was the doctor, apologizing for being delayed. I jumped up, ready to go to my room with him, but he told me, "No, take your time, I'm at your service, and again, I'm sorry about the delay. Tell the desk to call me when you are ready for me and I will come to the room to see you." The soup finally arrived and it was very good and did make me feel a little better.

A Moment in Time - Being treated by Dr. Rodovaldo

Doctors in Cuba are quite different from doctors in Canada. A Cuban doctor's medical training is completely paid for by the state, so when they are licenced, they are told where they will practice, and how many patients they must look after. They earn the same amount of money as other working people in the country, which is equal to about $20 a month.

    Back in our room, we called the desk, asking them to summon the doctor. Juan translated while I relayed my symptoms, telling the doctor that I thought I had become dehydrated in Parque Lenin. The doctor told us he practises a type of Chinese medicine, like acupuncture, combined with massage. He massaged my stomach and calves, and then gave me some medicine. He wrote out a diet to follow for the next few days, and told me to not hesitate to call him if I needed anything. He then went on to chat about Las Terrazas, asking us what we thought of the community and Hotel Moka. He made no mention of a fee, and when I offered, he covered his eyes saying he couldn't see me give him money, and then pointed to the pocket in his white coat. I placed 50 CUC in the pocket and thanked him for his kindness.

    Juan and Carene made plans to meet later for dinner and I went back to bed. The rest of the night was kind of a blur, but I was aware of Carene leaving the room then returning a while later, telling me Juan had stood her up. The phone rang and it was Juan apologizing profusely, telling Carene he had fallen asleep and he would be right up. After the day he had put in, it didn't surprise me that he had fallen asleep. Apparently he received quite a scolding from the woman at the desk for keeping Carene waiting.

    The next morning I was awakened early by a phone call from the doctor asking how I was. I was feeling a little better and even managed to eat breakfast. We went for a walk to check out the Polo Montanez museum, located in the home where Polo resided in Las Terrazas. A young woman from the community acted as a guide, showing us through. There were pictures and memorabilia displayed throughout the house and some of his CDs were available to purchase. Polo's older brother was also there to answer questions. It was evident how much Polo was loved and respected in the community.

*Polo Montanez was born in 1955 in the Cuban countryside, in a place called El Brugito. When Polo was ten he joined his father's small band, and learned how to play many instruments. Above all, music was for him, a family matter. Polo had practically never left his mountain home, and the music he played didn't sound like any other on the island.

He started to work from a very early age, and over the years he held many different jobs; e.g. assisting on the farm, driving tractors, and milking the cows; later, he became a lumberjack, which meant long hours and backbreaking work. But when night came, he always dedicated himself to his craft, going from house to house singing. In 1994, Polo gave up the saw and the axe to play full-time, and he started working in a deluxe hotel in Las Terrazas where he quickly became the regular house act. Polo was a very humble man. As well as being a simple yet profound poet, he created music that cannot be classified in the traditional music sense but is full of the strength of his elders and has nothing to do with fleeting trends that come and go every day.

Polo Montanez died as a result of a traffic accident when he was returning by car from the capital to his home in San Cristobal, Pinar del Río province.

We decided to have lunch at El Romero, the vegetarian restaurant. Juan explained my problem, and also told them we didn't have a great deal of time to wait for food. The owner and chef suggested something that would be easy on my stomach and it did taste good. The menu looked amazing and I knew I had to revisit Las Terrazas so that I could partake in all it had to offer.

Chapter Nine

We had made dinner plans with Jesús and a few others from Muraleando. I'm afraid it was the last thing I felt like doing, but I willed myself to not cancel. We did manage to enjoy dinner together and took lots of pictures. I thanked Jesús for all he had done for us, and through my tears assured them that I would be back next year

    I usually don't want to leave Cuba, but because I hadn't been well for much of the trip, I was looking forward to home. When I boarded the plane I told the flight attendant, "I usually look much better than this." She laughed and said, "That must mean you had a good time." Little did she know!

Bonnie Martin

Observations and Reflections - 2010

I know there are many places on earth that are beautiful, but when you are fortunate enough to experience a place that is not only beautiful, but also touches your heart, you can consider yourself to be one of the luckiest people there are.

Although the people of Cuba struggle, you can't help but notice a feeling of peace in the way a lot of them lead their lives. You feel as though you've been transported back to a time when life was simpler. They don't worry about how green their lawn is, or if they have the latest electronic gadget, and they certainly don't sweat the small stuff.

Las Terrazas is a wonder to behold. It is a place where people once led a very difficult life. Someone had a vision, and it was turned into a beautiful and peaceful community, where people who are lucky enough to call it home lead an idyllic life.

Some people believe that the people of Cuba are oppressed because they live under a socialist government. What I have witnessed are people who live life to the fullest and are basically quite happy.

July 2010

Chapter Ten

Because I had been ill for much of my trip in April, when the opportunity arose to return with my friends, Julie and Richard, I jumped at the chance.

We were going to be in Cuba for nine days, with Jesús and Juan as our guides. The first few days would be spent in Havana, and then we were taking a road trip to Viñales and Las Terrazas. We rented a car, which was a fabulous idea. Renting a car in Cuba isn't easy, nor is finding your way around, because there isn't an abundance of signage, so Juan would travel with us to alleviate any problems.

I arranged casas for us at 21 & O, where Carene and I had stayed in May. Julie and Richard would stay with Adelaida, and I would stay one floor above in Casa Teresita, owned by a lovely couple, Lincoln and his wife. When I returned to the casa in the afternoons, Lincoln always offered me café. His words to me one day were, "We like you very much, you come back, okay?"

As I have mentioned before, the angels work in mysterious ways. When we arrived in Cuba on July 25, I had no idea that July 26 is one of the country's biggest and most celebrated holidays. It commemorates the date in 1953 when one hundred and sixty Cuban rebels, led by Fidel Castro and Che Guevera, attacked the Moncada Barracks near Santiago de Cuba, trying to overthrow Batista. The raid failed but, because of it, the Revolution began. People get a two-day holiday, and it is also carnival time, making it an exciting time to visit. Cuban flags of various sizes can be seen hanging from balconies all over the city. Because I had missed the May Day celebrations, it seemed this trip was meant to be.

Jesús was waiting for us when we arrived, to help us get settled and show me to my casa. He told us there was going to be a concert that night and asked if we would like to attend. He said Juan and Maria were waiting down in the lobby, and since Jenny was staying with her cousin for the night, they were free. We hadn't planned on doing much our first night, but we accepted the invitation.

It had become a tradition for me to begin my holiday with mojitos at the Hotel Nacional, so we all walked across the street to get the evening started. We sat out at the edge of the rock and, with mojitos in hand, toasted being in beautiful Cuba.

The concert venue was too far to walk, so Jesús convinced a taxi driver with one of the old cars to take us. The driver was having second thoughts when we all piled in, but Jesús told him jokingly, we're all in the car now, and we're not leaving. The concert was small and intimate, mainly attended by local people. At one point during the performance, a small group of people entered the venue and things came to a halt. Jesús told us that one of the people was the Minister of Culture. He said this man was younger than most officials in the government, and had been chosen to try and bring new life to the arts.

Jesús and Lazaro picked us up for a day of touring. We drove through Vedado and Miramar, and then on to Fuster's, the famous ceramic artist. Making our way back to Havana, we visited Hammel's Alley, and were lucky enough to meet the main artist there, Salvador. One of the perks of having Jesús as a guide is he knows a lot of artists in and around Havana, so when we are with him, sometimes we get preferred treatment.

After lunch at a paladar, we went on a walking tour around Old Havana. The July heat was very intense and draining, so we didn't last long. While searching for water, we heard someone call to Jesús - it was Victor, (the tall one), an artist from Muraleando, sitting in a café with his new wife of fifteen days. Since congratulations were in order, we took the opportunity to join them for a drink and to cool down.

Today, we were visiting Muraleando, and because I had gifts for everyone we went directly to Manolo's house. Mario and Martin were there and, after visiting, we all walked over to the Boulevard of Friendship. Martin acted as a tour guide, pointing out different murals and sculptures. Very close to the Boulevard of Friendship was an old water tank that had been given to the Muraleando project, now completely overgrown with brush and weeds. They were very excited about the gift and planned to turn it into a cultural centre. Looking at it, I had trouble imagining how it would all come about, but I've learned that in Cuba, anything is possible.

Mario had told me in April that he wanted me to see the home he was building, so after our tour he extended an invitation to us. When we arrived, two teenaged boys were there, and Mario said something about them being his helpers. He proudly ushered us in to his small home, with a front room, a kitchen and a bathroom. His bed was in the kitchen, but he explained his future plan of adding a bedroom, and a studio for his music, on a second level. After showing us around he began to cue up some music on an old computer, so I thought we were going to listen to some music. I have learned to just "go with the flow" in Cuba, so I didn't ask any questions.

A Moment in Time - A performance just for us

What followed was another case of me being clued out while in Cuba. When Mario said that the two boys were his helpers, I assumed they were helping him with the construction of his house.

As we all stood around, Mario explained while he'd been in jail, he had a lot of time to think about what he wanted to accomplish in his life. When he went to live in Muraleando, and the people were so good to him, he decided to pay it forward and help other young people from the barrio. He went on to explain that in Cuba they don't have baseball diamonds or soccer fields in every barrio, so without much to do, it's easy for young people to get into trouble.

Mario had taken these two boys under his wing and introduced them to his life's passion, rap music. They had written a rap song that they were going to perform for us. Holding lotion bottles as faux microphones, they began. We all watched and grooved along with them. It was so special that it brought Julie to tears. She thanked each of the boys with a kiss.

Because so much goes on when I'm in Cuba, and with me being on an emotional high, I don't always realize what has taken place until I think about it later. That night as I drifted off to sleep, it occurred to me that the performance had been planned for us and I'm sure many hours of preparation had gone into the whole thing.

It was now time for Julie and Richard to experience one of Mayra's delicious lunches, so we said good-bye to Mario and Martin and made our way back to Manolo's. At lunch, Manolo relayed through Jesús, some of what he had experienced when he visited Canada the previous year. One thing that stood out was how many different nationalities live in Canada, and how tolerant we are of them all. Richard told him it was a nice sentiment, but not always true. Another one of his observations, which I found quite funny, was that we all barbequed a lot. We finished our lunch with some of Mayra's wonderful café and thanked them for the meal. We were going to Yosiet's for a visit, and then Manolo would pick us up and drive us back to our casas.

Yosiet now had three people working with him. He was selling his art in flea markets, and because he purposely sells items the average Cuban can afford, he was achieving success. Yosiet is a very kind and giving person, with emotions that run deep. Whenever I visit, he not only is a wonderful host, he usually gives gifts of his work, or tokens of friendship. While we looked around the studio, he disappeared, returning with a gorgeous plate he had made, telling me it was a gift for Carene. The gesture was so unexpected, it brought me to tears.

We went outside to wait for Manolo, and as we stood chatting, the topic of José Martí came up. Yosiet disappeared yet again, returning with an antique book of Martí's writings and gave it to Richard. At first Richard didn't want to accept the gift, telling Yosiet he should give to his son, but after some persuasion, he relented and accepted. Manolo arrived so we said our good-byes with me promising to see them next year.

Chapter Eleven

We were travelling to Viñales, so Richard met Juan in Old Havana where they picked up the rental car. Our plan was to drive directly to Viñales by the main highway, then, on the way back toward Las Terrazas take a scenic route along the north coast. Renting a car allowed us to see parts of Cuba we would never have seen had we travelled by bus.

About an hour out of Havana we stopped at a rest stop for lunch. They offered a variety of blender drinks, with or without rum, and since Julie and I weren't driving we had ours with. While we sat eating, the gentleman who made our drinks came to our table and plopped a bottle of rum down, telling us, "In case you don't have enough." Only in Cuba!

We arrived at Purry's and got ourselves settled. She had other guests, so Julie and Richard would stay with her and I would stay at the casa next door. We'd all dine together in Purry's lovely outdoor dining area. Because I had only been able to eat a small amount of her chicken on my last visit, I requested it for our dinner.

We walked to the end of the main street to visit Benito's tobacco farm. The farmer was busy with another customer, and because it had begun to rain again, we took cover on the arcade at the front of the family home. When the rain stopped the children came out of the house and proceeded to run and slide in the mud, laughing with glee, until their mother quickly put a stop to it, scolding them. She saw us laughing and turned and smiled, but kept her stern façade for the children.

When the farmer finished with his other visitor we made our way into the drying shed. It was Benito's son who explained things to us, and he was a charmer – a rugged-looking man with skin that was brown and leathered from years of sun exposure. His eyes were very dark, with a friendly twinkle, and his straw hat completed the look.

The drying shed was empty of tobacco leaves, but he explained the drying process, and gave us a demonstration of how a cigar is rolled.

We were all offered a cigar, which Richard accepted and enjoyed with the farmer. Julie purchased some cigars then we made our way into the house for café.

Juan asked about Benito and was told he had experienced some health problems, so for him to recuperate properly, they had him staying away from the farm, to stop him from working. I had brought some photos I had taken in May and gave them to Benito's wife. The gesture seemed to please them, and the farmer gave me a gift of cigars in return.

Back up the street we found a small patio with a few musicians playing. Every time I hear music in Cuba, I'm amazed by the talent. Here we were, in a small town on a Wednesday afternoon, listening to fantastic live music. Life was good. Because we were a good audience, the band seemed to enjoy us almost as much as we were enjoying them. Musicians in Cuba aren't paid by the venue but make their money from tips and the sale of their CDs. The CDs aren't always the best quality, but they are reasonably priced, so I purchased one. It turned out to be one of my favourite CDs from Cuba.

We freshened up and then sat down to a wonderful chicken dinner. Richard commented that never again would he say that the food in Cuba isn't very good. Sitting in Purry's outdoor dining area with the air fresh after the rain was sublime. We had planned to continue our evening at the Polo Montanez club in the town square but I was fading fast. It had been a long day so I relented, saying I thought I was going to call it a night. When I said that, Julie thought she would do the same, leaving Richard and Juan to go out on their own.

Over breakfast, we made a plan for our second day in Viñales. Richard thought we could go to a town on the water to have some beach time, but a young man visiting Purry told us Juan wouldn't be allowed, because there is a ferry boat at the location. As Juan put it, Cubans and boats don't mix. We opted instead for a town on the seaside that Juan could visit.

We reached the shore and found a long pier with people swimming and enjoying the day. There was a nice park area and an outdoor pavilion where food and drinks could be purchased. It seemed like a very nice spot for people to spend time near the water, and a lot of people were doing just that.

Back in Viñales we went to the botanical gardens, and then lunched in one of the few restaurants in Viñales, Casa de Don Tomás.

*Casa de Don Tomás is a minor architectural gem, built in 1887-88 for Gerardo Miel y Sainz, a rich merchant and agent for a shipping line. The building was restored in 1991 and turned into a good fish restaurant.

After dinner that night, we ventured down the street to the Polo Montanez Club where there was going to be a floor show, and later, a band. We managed a good table just off the dance floor, and Richard began pointing out a few people of interest, one of them being a madam. The club is frequented by ladies, men, couples, and also transvestites. The transvestites and some of the ladies are under the direction of the madam, who will offer pretty much anything one would like. Apparently, the night before, Richard had received a few offers. When Juan had relayed the story to us over breakfast, he kept saying, "Julie, he loves you, he really loves you."

The floor show was very good, with Afro-Cuban dancers, complete with fire-eaters. When it was over, the band came on stage and dancing began. Juan loves to dance and had been trying to teach me how to salsa, so we got up. I always feel so inept dancing in Cuba because the locals do it so well. I find the footwork pretty easy, but there are a lot of intricate arm movements, along with turns and spins, which are a whole different story. Juan is a very good teacher, and as he guided me, I almost felt like a pro. The mojitos I'd been drinking helped me get in the groove.

When Juan went to the bar for drinks, he came back to the table chuckling and told us a funny story. He said the madam had approached him asking about Richard, wondering if he would be interested in a date. Juan told her no, Richard was quite happy with the woman he was with. We laughed thinking it quite funny, but apparently Julie didn't find it all that humorous. When we got up to leave and headed toward the exit, Julie turned and went in the opposite direction. We thought she must be going to the ladies room, but instead, she went over to the madam and spoke to her. When she returned and we inquired what had taken place, she said she told the madam, "Just so you know, he's with me!" Both Richard and Juan had a look of disbelief on their faces, and I thought I would die laughing. We hustled Julie out of the club. We laughed all the way back to Purry's, and Juan and I have laughed about the incident many times since.

It was time to say good-bye to Viñales. Because we were taking the back roads to Las Terrazas, we were in for a long drive, but looking forward to it.

A Moment in Time - The best pineapple I've ever eaten

We came upon a gazebo at the foot of a driveway, with a man and woman selling fruit. We wanted mangos, but theirs didn't seem to be ripe enough. Julie and I still hadn't learned to, as they say, "stop and smell the roses", so we went back to the car. Richard and Juan stayed at the fruit stand, and I could see the man in a field beside the stand trimming a pineapple. I assumed Juan was taking one home for Mari, but when he began trimming another one, Julie and I went to see what was going on.

He made himself a handle out of the spines, then holding the *piña,* sliced off the skin, trimmed it nicely, and then cut it up, placing the pieces on a paper plate. In the meantime, his wife ran up the hill to their home, returning with a basin of water that she placed on a pedestal beside the gazebo. She disappeared again, this time returning with a paper plate containing some coarse salt. Juan explained it was the added touch, telling us that Cubans sometimes put salt on their pineapple. I came to the conclusion that the Cuban people, who seem to know a lot about health through nature, do it as a way of replenishing their electrolytes. With the pineapple prepared, we were told to dig in. There were groans of pleasure all around and we agreed this was as good as it gets. It was warm from the sun, at the peak of ripeness, sweet and juicy. I tried a piece with salt, but preferred it plain. When we finished our tasty treat, we were directed to the basin of water to wash up. We asked what we owed and the amount equalled about 21¢. Julie and I each gave the woman 2 CUC, feeling the whole experience was well worth it.

As we drove through a small town, looking for a place for lunch, a young man standing on a corner flagged us down telling us his house was a paladar. When we arrived, we found a family of four already there waiting for lunch. What we didn't realize was our meals wouldn't be prepared until after we ordered them, which took over an hour. Not only had we wasted a lot of time, but the meal was mediocre.

One good thing that came out of our stop was some advice about reaching Las Terrazas. The man of the house told us the road we were planning on taking was in very poor condition, and mainly only used by large trucks. He added that it would rip the bottom off our car. Even though the route he suggested was about twenty miles out of the way, we heeded his advice.

After we arrived in Las Terrazas, we checked into our rooms and got situated. Time was getting on, so thinking we'd better find some dinner while things were still open, we went to El Romero, the vegetarian restaurant. El Romero is a first-class restaurant where I have eaten many times since, and can't believe a restaurant of this calibre is located in such an out-of-the-way place.

The next day, Juan and I went to find Doctor Rodovaldo, who had treated me in May. I had some meds for him, and I wanted to invite him to join us for dinner. Juan told his nurse why we were there, and in between patients she spoke with the doctor. He was quite surprised to see us and after chatting for a few moments, I extended the dinner invitation to him. He suggested we go to Fonda de Mercedes, which serves traditional Cuban food, and according to the locals, is the best place to eat in Las Terrazas.

One of the places I wanted to visit in Las Terrazas was the biosphere reserve. I had to cancel a tour last trip, and because we had arrived late, I was unable to book it the day before. It seemed it just wasn't meant to be. Instead, we decided to go to the Río San Juan.

Arriving at the river, we were met with a thing of beauty. Walkways of natural stone led from the parking lot and, after crossing a bridge over the river, continued through a lovely picnic area amongst the trees. Tables with mosaic tops, and cut logs sitting upright for seats, were here and there. The walkway continued to a kiosk selling drinks and snacks, and then to a large open-air restaurant called El Bambu. Behind the picnic area were cabanas on stilts, with thatched roofs, for people wanting to camp. Horseback riding was also available, making it seem like they had thought of everything to make the park a place for people to enjoy. The cost to use all the facilities was 2 CUC, less for Cuban people, and free for guests of the Hotel Moka.

It was a Saturday and close to the July 26 holiday, so the park was full of people. Coolers held food and cold drinks, and a lot of rum was being consumed.

The main attraction amidst the beauty is the river, flowing through the area, over rocks made smooth with moss, making fantastic natural water slides. Small waterfalls flow into pools where you can sit and feel the water flow past, like a natural Jacuzzi. At one spot the river flows over large rocks then drops in elevation, forming a large swimming pool.

While we swam, one of the many dogs living in the park came and stood beside the river, looking like he wanted to cool off. He jumped in and had a swim, but then had difficulty getting out. He struggled, trying to climb up the rocks, but the moss was making it impossible for him to get his footing. Two young ladies sitting on the edge of the rocks leaned over, grabbed the dog by his front legs, and pulled him out. He shook himself then turned and happily walked away.

After our swim Julie went for a walk and came back quite excited, telling Richard he had to go with her to see something. She had come upon an outdoor grill where a man was cooking various pieces of pork and chicken, which we thought would make a nice lunch. Richard and Juan went and ordered some meat, telling the cook there were four of us. He suggested an appropriate piece of pork, and told them to return in a few minutes and lunch would be ready. The cost for the entire meal would be 20 CUC. They returned with three plates, heaped with pieces of carved pork, complete with crackling. Along with the pork were another four plates containing morro and some french fries. We ate and ate, not even emptying one plate of pork. We fed the dogs from the park until they were full, and still had a lot of pork left. Juan walked around offering some to different people, but because everyone had their own food, there were no takers. We couldn't bear to throw two full plates of meat away, so Juan went back to the cook, got a plastic bag, and we took the meat with us so Juan could give it to his host family.

We were dumbfounded by the amount of meat we had received. When Richard asked Juan why we were sold so much pork, his reply was simply, "Cubans like to eat a lot of pork." Richard quipped that when his friends at home ask him what he did in Cuba he'd say, "Oh, I just sat around and ate about nine pounds of pork for lunch."

What a wonderful day we had. Upon reflection I realized that if we had taken the tour to the bio reserve, I would have missed experiencing the river. The angels do work in mysterious ways.

A Moment in Time - Juan and the Río San Juan

Whenever we visit Las Terrazas, Juan's sister asks him to bring her a bottle of water from the river. When I inquired about this, he told me she adds the water to her bath.

On one visit, Juan and I went to the river for lunch. After, we sat with our feet in the water, taking in the beauty around us. As we were getting ready to leave, Juan said, "Just let me go and say hello to the river." I stayed where I was and watched as he went and squatted, then took some water and splashed it on his face. He then filled an empty bottle with water to take to his sister.

I wasn't sure what properties they feel the river holds, but knew it is sacred to them. After witnessing Juan having his quiet time with the river I asked him to explain it. I will write it as it was told to me:

> Religion in Cuba is very strong. When the highest level of earth receives the rain, it causes a current of water to come down from the mountains where it is filtered through the rocks and soil. People use the water for cleansing themselves from bad spirits, and to receive good spirits. People who live a distance from the river will ask someone who is visiting it to bring them some water to add to their bath. I, (Juan) have witnessed people in other rivers, naked, cleansing their bodies with herbs and the water. In the Santería religion, this is all supervised by a Godfather.

The more I thought about the whole thing, it all made sense. For thousands of years, people the world over have gone to rivers to cleanse themselves and to be baptized. Water can symbolize life itself. It is important in rituals in many religions in the world.

After a cocktail in the hotel bar, we made our way down the hill to meet the doctor for dinner. He is quite shy, so initially things were a little awkward, but before long we were all relaxed and having a good time. Juan sat at the head of the table and was right on his game translating, so conversation flowed easily. The doctor explained a little about the form of Chinese medicine he practises, and told us some of the ways the medical profession in Cuba differs from ours. Cuban doctors are assigned a set number of patients and they are expected to visit them in their homes a certain number of times a year. He went on to explain that one of his duties is to teach people the importance of the use of clean water. Care must be taken, especially in spring, because water has been basically sitting during the winter months. They need heavy spring rain, allowing water to run down from the mountains to cleanse the rivers and land. He said when I had become ill, it was perhaps due to bad water.

On a subsequent visit to Las Terrazas when I stayed in community housing, I witnessed the family washing their dishes. They cleaned them under running water, not in a sink full of soapy water as most of us do. To me it seemed like a waste of water, but when I asked Juan about it he assured me it is one of the things they are taught by doctors to assure cleanliness.

We said good-bye to Las Terrazas and returned to Havana for our last night in Cuba.

I took Juan, Jesús, and his family to dinner while Richard and Julie ventured into Old Havana. I met everyone at La Rocha, and, although the company was good, the meal and atmosphere were disappointing. We said our good-byes and I told them hopefully, I would see them again in 2011.

More Observations and Reflections - 2010

Drivers in Havana have nerves of steel and a keen sense of alertness. People constantly cross the streets in front of cars, never seeming to be in a hurry. My assumption is because of the heat and the relaxed attitude of the Cuban people, no one seems to be in a hurry.

In Viñales most people keep chickens in their yards, and many seem to go for a daily walk in the neighbourhood. They peck in the grass beside the road, and when they're finished, return to where they came from.

In Las Terrazas, not only do chickens, dogs and cats roam free, but horses do as well. Come to think of it, if I were a horse, I wouldn't leave such a beautiful place.

Cuban people use plants and herbs in many ways for their health. When I came upon two women cleaning a big pot of green beans, they told me green beans are good for your skin and eyes. We had been eating them by the plateful, usually served icy cold, sometimes with vinegar, and sometimes plain with cucumbers or avocados.

Cuba is known for high-quality rum, usually drunk neat by the local people. According to Juan, it's the ice that gives you headaches.

Acts of kindness seem to come naturally to Cuban people, toward both people and animals. Witnessing them always touches me deeply.

Section Five

Feb/Mar 2011

Rio San Juan, Las Terrazas – 2011

El Tanque, Muraleando – 2011

My Love Affair with Cuba

Manolo, Bonnie, Jesús, Mayra, Erminda, Muraleando – 2011

Bonnie Martin

People You'll Meet

Julieta Leon - Artist

Chapter Twelve

In 2011, our family would celebrate the marriage of our daughter Carene, and for that reason she wouldn't be accompanying me to Cuba. I wasn't about to let a little thing like a wedding stop me, so I asked my sister-in-law, Anne, if she would be interested in experiencing Cuba.

A lot of what we would do would be things I had done and seen, but it would be fun to share the experience with Anne. We would spend a few days in Havana, travel to Viñales and Las Terrazas, and then back to Havana.

Jesús and Juan were there to meet us when we arrived at the casa, and after getting settled, we took a walk on the Malecón toward Old Havana to have dinner. A leisurely walk beside the water proved to be a good introduction to Cuba for Anne.

On this day we were going to Muraleando, and as always, I was excited to see everyone again. Most of the artists were there when we arrived and we received a warm welcome. Because I knew Muraleando was working on their new project, *El Tanque*, I gave Manolo a card with a donation. Richard and Julie had also sent a donation for Muraleando, which they were very grateful to receive.

El Tanque

Muraleando had received a gift of an old water tank (circa 1911) from the municipality of October Tenth and their plan was to turn it into a cultural centre. I had first laid eyes on the tank in July 2010, where it sat atop a small rise, completely overgrown with trees and scrub.

The first thing done was the removal of sixty-four truckloads of dirt and debris. Windows and a large door were made using jack hammers to conquer the thick concrete wall. Two jack hammers were broken.

Manolo wanted us to walk over to El Tanque to see the work in progress. Men were inside on scaffolding, chipping cement away from metal beams in the ceiling to expose them for structural reasons. I was horrified to see the men doing the chipping wore no safety glasses. Here they were at ceiling height, looking up, using a small jackhammer, with cement flying everywhere, but no one seemed at all concerned. Outside, some were constructing a kiln, while others did more excavating, as well as landscaping.

As we walked amidst piles of dirt and debris, Manolo told us how fortunate they were to receive the gift of the tank, and what they hoped to accomplish. I'm afraid I wasn't as optimistic as he was, but Cubans are used to overcoming many obstacles, and not afraid of hard work, so Manolo had every right to be optimistic.

When it was time for lunch we went back to Manolo's where Mayra was working her magic in the kitchen. At lunch, Manolo told us there would be a tenth birthday celebration for Muraleando the next day at a social club in Miramar, and they would love for us to attend. Not only was I happy to receive the invitation, I was pleased that Anne could be a part of their celebration.

Mario had finished his work at El Tanque for the day, so he came to Manolo's for a visit. Every year I give one person an extra special gift, and this year I was giving it to Mario, to help with the construction of his house. Richard and Julie had also sent some gifts for him and he was very pleased by both gestures of friendship.

I had arranged to take the Lazaro family out for dinner, but since Lazaro was ill with a kidney infection, they were unable to go. Instead, they invited us to their home for a visit.

Although I had tried to warn Anne that reaching the Lazaro's home is a bit difficult, there are just some things you can't prepare someone for. This was the first tenement building she had been in, and even though there are many far worse, I think she was still unprepared.

While we visited, I was feeling sorry for Lazaro, as I could tell he wasn't well at all. His colour was bad and he was fevered. He probably would have rather been in bed, but he was a trooper and hung in with us. We heard all about Melina's fifteenth birthday party, and it sounded like it had been a huge success, beginning at six in the evening and lasting until ten the next morning. Lazaro had taken all of the photos, and they said because I had given him the camera, it enabled them to save money on a photographer. I was told to pick out some pictures as a gift, which I thought was very sweet.

We were going to tour Old Havana with Jesús before the birthday party for Muraleando. Jesús arranged to have us picked up near his friend Victor's home so that we could give him a ride to the party. We arrived in Miramar before the bus from Muraleando, so we waited across the road in a small park. Victor had brought his guitar, and he played and sang a song for us. It was another one of those moments I am lucky enough to experience while in Cuba.

The bus arrived with the artists, along with their families and some friends. I met Mario's little daughter, and Nivia proudly introduced me to her grandson. He was so cute, wearing little blue jeans with a chain going from his waist to a pocket, a religious medal around his neck, a gold bracelet and a small angel pin on his back shoulder. I inquired about the pin and was told it was protection from "bad eyes". I interpreted it as a guardian angel on his shoulder.

As we entered the building, Anne and I were told to get into the middle of the group and to not speak English until we got upstairs. The club is only open to Cubans, and there were security guards at the door. The party room was large and set up with rows of long tables. Music began playing, and immediately the little girls in the crowd were dancing. Jugs of beer, rum and soft drinks were served and it didn't take long before the party was in full swing.

There is a fellow from Muraleando, who I refer to as The One Man Band. He built himself a contraption by welding steel and attaching various things used for percussion instruments that he plays with drum sticks. Attached are two old bicycle wheels, enabling him to transport it to various functions easily. His enthusiasm while he plays makes any party come alive.

A Moment in Time - Manolo arrives

Well into the party, Manolo still hadn't arrived. For some reason he was driving his car to the party, and word had it he was having car trouble. Just as we were having appetizers, there was a commotion outside the room, then, in walked Manolo, dressed as a woman. He wore a dress with a red bra strap showing, ankle socks with flip-flop sandals, lots of jewellery and was carrying a purse. His wig, eye make-up and bright red lips completed his look. He had a glass of water, containing a set of dentures in his hand, and said "she" had just come in from Muraleando, and was looking for her husband. Holding up the dentures, she said they were all he had left behind. Someone in the crowd yelled out, "Shave your legs!" As you can imagine, the room erupted with gales of laughter and I thought Mayra, who obviously knew nothing about the whole thing, would die laughing. How Manolo had kept it all a secret, I'll never know.

A big birthday cake was brought out, and everyone gathered around to sing Happy Birthday. There were tickets for draws given out for gifts that had been donated by the artists. It was a fun day of celebration that I was honoured to have been included in.

A Moment in Time - Witnessing a cat fight

Lazaro was picking us up and had parked on a side street to wait for us. Sitting in the car, ready to leave, we heard some shouting coming from across the street. Two young women were pushing and shoving each other while some men tried to separate them. They were attracting attention, so people were doing their best to get them out of the street. When the excitement was over, Victor casually told us the fight was over a man. With that, Maria looked at me, shrugged her shoulders and said, "That's Cuba."

Chapter Thirteen

Today, we were taking the bus to Viñales, and when we made a rest stop in Las Terrazas, unfortunately, Anne got sick. We checked in to Purry's and got Anne situated in her room so she could lie down for a while. She told Juan and me to go and have some lunch, and she would be fine.

We learned there was going to be a concert at the Polo Montanez Club later that afternoon. Anne was still nauseous but assured me there was nothing I could do, so go and have a good time.

A Sunday afternoon in Viñales

Juan and I walked into the Polo Montanez Cultural Centre, paid the 50¢ admission, and found a table close to the large open-air dance floor. A stage at the front was set up with instruments, but at that time, recorded music was playing.

As I looked around, taking in the surroundings, I was seeing Cuban life at its finest. On the outer edges of the dance floor tables were set up and they were full. In front of us three older women sat chatting, other tables held families, out for a Sunday afternoon together, and at others there were young couples and groups of people. Some young teens arrived and they were struttin' their stuff. The girls wore sunglasses, not to shield their eyes from the sun, but placed just so on top of their heads as a fashion statement. A young couple showed off their new baby, dressed to the nines, right down to her tiny pink shoes. Quite a few people approached them, fussing over the baby, so I assumed this was her debut.

Juan learned the headliners were from Puerto Rico, but some local talent would also perform. The concert began with a female singer who sang a few numbers, and then introduced different acts. Whenever she returned to the stage, it was always with a costume change. The headlining band did a few numbers then brought out a guitar player who reminded me of Carlos Santana. Two young rap artists were next, and the young people in the crowd loved them. When they did the Spanish version of a song by Queen with some off-colour lyrics inserted, they went over to the table of older ladies and apologized. Different acts performed and then the amateurs began to be introduced. At one point, a young man from Pinar del Río came on, and before he began he told the audience he hoped he didn't forget the lyrics like he had the last time. The music began and when he opened his mouth, out came a booming tenor voice. The room became silent and chills ran up my spine. When he finished his first number the female singer ran over and hugged him, asking if he wanted a job with her band. Once again, I was amazed by the musical talent in Cuba.

Anne's upset stomach had continued all afternoon so she wasn't going to eat dinner. The woman who cooks for Purry told us that after we ate, she would take us to the twenty-four hour clinic so Anne could get a shot to stop her nausea. At the clinic, after some preliminary questions, they took her blood pressure and then gave her a shot of Gravol mixed with B3 & B6. The doctor said she might be sick once more after the shot, not to drink for two hours, then take only sips of water or lemon-lime soda. Everything went exactly as he said it would, and by the following morning she was fine.

Anne was going to take it slow today. We visited Benito's tobacco farm and his son gave us a tour. As we walked back up the street, the town was a hive of activity. Many vendors were selling not only goods, but also an array of food. Lovely aromas wafted from a bakery, a barber had his chair on the front porch of his house and, on the porch of another house, six pregnant women sat relaxing in rocking chairs. Juan explained when women who are expecting have any complications they are moved to special houses so they can be monitored.

We ate lunch at Casa de Don Tomás, and then lingered on the upper veranda with Juan telling Anne a little about the Special Period and how difficult life had been then.

At the botanical gardens – my third visit – the guide recognized me, so traded places with another guide and showed us through.

It was time to relax with mojitos, so we found an outdoor café. There, we noticed a lineup at the counter and everyone seemed to be buying cookies. Cookies and snacks are quite expensive in Cuba, so we came to the conclusion there must be a sale going on. Even Juan couldn't contain himself and bought six packages to take home. He inquired and was told the best before date was about to expire, so the cookies were half price.

Some musicians arrived so we thought we'd have another drink while listening to some music. Anne decided she'd had enough so went back to Purry's. When I wanted a third drink, I had to twist Juan's arm to join me, but in the end he relented. He was pretty happy by the time we got back, and walking in the door he announced, "Purreeee, it's me Juan….I'm home….Bonnie made me drink another drink, so I'm kind of drunk."

We hired a Cuba Taxi to tour the area with Anne, showing her the caves, the prehistoric mural, and the look-out. We thought we should get something to eat before catching the bus to Las Terrazas. Only wanting something light, I ordered a tomato salad, and Anne ordered a mixed. Salad in Cuba is usually made with grated cabbage, sometimes with other vegetables added. Oil and vinegar are on the table and you mix it yourself. The waitress told me there were no tomatoes, so I opted for a mixed salad. What arrived were two plates of grated cabbage – that's it, that's all. As we both starred dumbfounded, Anne blurted out, "That's it?" All I could do was laugh.

Juan went to the bus station to purchase our tickets to Las Terrazas, returning a short time later, quite excited, telling us a Cuba Taxi would take us to Las Terrazas for the same cost as the bus. Because we wouldn't have to make a stop in Pinar del Río, we would arrive in Las Terrazas sooner. We agreed that sounded like a good plan, so Juan went back, telling us they would pick us up shortly. Anne and I were sitting on the porch waiting when a taxi drove by with Juan in it, looking quite embarrassed. Cuba Taxi is the largest taxi company in Cuba, with good cars, but the one Juan was in was a piece of junk. Anne asked if I thought the car would have air conditioning. I told her it probably wouldn't, but said when we got moving, and the windows open, we would be fine.

A Moment in Time - A ride from hell

We climbed into our ride, an old Lada, and not only did it not have air conditioning, it didn't have a lot of other things, including back windows that rolled down. It reeked of gas and was stifling hot. As we drove down the rough road to the highway, we were going a lot faster than I liked. The road has many curves, and with four people in the car and our luggage in the trunk, we hit bottom more than once. I kept telling myself that when we got to the highway it would be better. I stretched to look at the gauges to see how fast we were going, and not only did the gas gauge not work, neither did the speedometer. The smell of gas in the air was thick, making me think there was probably a hole in the tank. I was thinking I'd never survive the drive with such a strong odor, and at the same time wondering how Anne was managing. I remembered I had my trusty sweat rag in my purse, so I took it out, poured some water on it and held it to my face, which helped a little. When we arrived in Las Terrazas I was never so happy to reach my destination, but, my glee wouldn't last for long.

There was no one at the desk when we arrived, so we waited patiently, realizing we were on Cuba time. When the desk clerk came back and began to help us, she and Juan were deep in conversation, and there seemed to be a problem. Apparently, the doctor had called, asking her to let him know when we arrived which concerned her because we weren't on the reservation list, and she knew the hotel was fully booked.

She relayed that to Juan and he told her assuredly that we were booked into cabanas. That's when things began to go downhill.

When we had made our reservations, the Cuban travel agent told us the hotel was booked, but there were cabanas available. I thought she was talking about what I now know to be community housing. Cabanas are small cabins, located four kilometers from the hotel, beside the Río San Juan. They are on stilts, so you must climb a ladder to reach them. I knew there was no way we would get our suitcases up a ladder, and couldn't see myself climbing down in the middle of the night to make a trip to the outdoor *baño*. We weren't prepared for camping, so staying in a cabana was out of the question.

I told Juan we had to head back to Havana. He needed to find out if there was a taxi available to take us, and if not, we'd have to hustle to meet the bus that would arrive from Viñales in about half an hour. A taxi agreed to take us, so I began to relax a little. Juan placed a call to Jesús, who wasn't home, but he did reach Maria. She went to work and arranged rooms for us at 21 & O.

The doctor called, excited to see us. When Juan told him about the mix-up he said he would come to the hotel directly for a quick visit. He arrived with a sad look on his face, and seemed embarrassed, telling us he felt the mix-up was a reflection on Cuba, and that we were going to think ill of them. I assured him it was all right – just a lack of communication. He even had a discussion with the desk clerk about getting us rooms and was told there was nothing she could possibly do. Later, she asked Juan if we could take the doctor to Havana with us to get him off her back. With some time at our disposal, we all went to the bar and had some drinks. The doctor was on duty and had to leave to see to some patients, but he did return. We visited a while longer but I knew we were keeping him from his work, so I paid the bill, telling him we should leave. We said our good-byes and I promised I would see him again.

Chapter Fourteen

At 21 & O, Anne stayed with Adelaida and I stayed in a casa I hadn't been in before. Located in one of the grandest apartments in the building, the room was lovely and even had a private entrance.

Because our plans had changed dramatically, I wasn't sure what we would be doing the next couple of days, but again, I put my trust in Jesús. He and Juan picked us up, telling us we were going to visit two ceramic artists. One, a woman I had never met, Julieta Leon, and then we would visit Fuster's property.

Julieta lives in a tiny two-storey home situated right on the ocean. We approached the locked gate and Jesús called out to her in the familiar Cuban way. A ceramic tiled walk, lined with potted plants, led to a small room that acted as a sitting room, a kitchen, as well as a studio. The kitchen counter and backsplash were decorated with Julieta's hand-painted tiles, and the walls held large oil paintings also done by her. The kitchen stove acted as her kiln. When I asked to use the washroom, I was directed to climb ladder-type stairs against one wall. The second floor held two very small bedrooms and an equally tiny bathroom, and at the front was a balcony with a gorgeous view of the ocean. Jesús said that she had pretty well re-built the house, and considering the shape it had been in when he first saw it she had done a great job. Julieta lives with her teenaged son, and told us that she doesn't have good luck with men. I told her with her pretty house, her son, and her cute puppy that we had met on the way in, she didn't need a man.

Back in Old Havana, we had lunch and then Anne and I walked around, exploring at our own pace. When we came upon the chocolate museum I suggested we go in. As soon as we entered, I heard my name being called and realized it was Manolo and Mayra's daughter, who is employed there. She greeted us, and suggested we sit in the courtyard. She then spoke with our waitress, who escorted us to a table. We ordered a cold chocolate drink. Served in a tall glass, it came with two cookies: one milk chocolate and one dark chocolate. The drink was absolutely delicious. Not thick like our chocolate milk, it wasn't too sweet, but ice cold and very refreshing. When I went to pay, the waitress told me it had been taken care of, as a thank you from Manolo's daughter for the gifts I had given them over the years. As we were leaving, I made sure to go and thank her. Since Anne hadn't been in a cocotaxi, we found one to take us back to our casas.

Juan would be our guide for the day, with plans to tour the cigar factory, and then take in a baseball game. At the cigar factory, Juan arranged for an English tour; he would meet up with us later. During the tour a funny thing happened that made me smile. Because of the bad press Cuba receives, some are under the impression that the people are mistreated, so consequently assume the cigar factory is run like a sweat shop. Nothing could be farther from the truth. When a British woman asked the guide how many days a week, and how many hours a day the people work, she answered, "Five days, Monday to Friday from seven a.m. to five p.m.", in a way that said, "Why would you ask?"

When Jesús suggested that Anne and I should go to a baseball game, I was a little leery. I pictured us sitting on some rustic benches in the middle of a field with the sun blazing down on us. With baseball being Cuba's most popular sport, I certainly should have known better. You'd think with this being my seventh time visiting Cuba, I would have more faith in their way of doing things.

A Moment in Time - An afternoon baseball game

The stadium was large and not unlike ones I was used to, but with one big difference – the price of admission. At the window for tourists, Anne and I paid 3 CUC each, while Juan paid much less, in Cuban pesos. For that price we had seats on the first base line, seven rows back. The home team (Havana) was playing a team from one of the eastern provinces, which happened to be Juan's home town. With the game in the second inning the excitement had already begun. Havana had been on a losing

My Love Affair with Cuba

streak so some fans were holding up signs, one reading, "The lion isn't dead – he was just sleeping." I heard some shouting near us and looked over to see two men standing, gesturing and yelling at each other. I thought a fight was about to break out, but Juan smiled, telling me they were just emotional fans. A young boy sitting in front of us had a pile of notebooks and was keeping stats. Whenever the home team was at bat, a band played, and people stood and danced. Another thing that stood out was the bat boys – not boys, but middle-aged men, and not in the best physical condition. Juan explained that in Cuba, being asked to be a bat boy is an honour.

Vendors sold a variety of items: popcorn, bubble gum, guava jelly, peanuts, stick candy, balloons and café. The café was sold in a unique way. A vendor carried a large stainless steel kettle and small plastic glasses, and when a café was ordered, it would be poured at the seat. Juan told us that rum isn't allowed in the stadium, but people do sneak it in. It was a good game with Havana being victorious.

On our last full day in Cuba, we told Jesús we wanted to spend time outside, before returning to the Canadian cold. We were going to Necrópolis Colón, Havana's cemetery, and then to Casablanca.

Because Necrópolis Colón is so large (135 acres), it was necessary to raise admission to 5 CUC from 1 CUC, to help with the cost of maintaining the grounds. We walked all around the main section where the older tombs are located while Jesús related the legends and stories pertaining to them. I told him I wanted to visit the tomb of Amelia Goyri, The Miraculous One, who grants miracles. My friend Marilyn was very ill with cancer, so I wanted to ask for a miracle. Next, we drove to the section where the cremated remains of citizens of modest means are stored. For 10 Cuban pesos a year, cremated remains are kept in numbered boxes until the family can afford a burial plot. Jesús had lost his father a few months previous, and this was where he was resting. Jesús asked if he could visit his father saying, "I just want to say hello to him." We waited in the car to give him some privacy, and I was moved when I witnessed him on his knees paying his respects.

Lazaro drove us to the ferry that would take us to Casablanca and we said our good-byes to him. In Casablanca we went to a café beside the water for some refreshments and I got a little cocky, and ordered a fresh guava juice. Soon after arriving home I came to regret it, realizing the juice had probably been made with regular water. A lesson learned – remain vigilant at all times, especially where water is concerned.

I was taking Juan, Jesús and a few people from Muraleando out to dinner for our last night. Jesús and Juan were at the restaurant when we arrived, so we had some private time with them. We ordered drinks, and then exchanged some gifts before my guests from Muraleando arrived.

Apparently the service wasn't up to par, but I was having so much fun I was oblivious to the problem. After we ate, I saw a man speaking with Manolo, and it was obvious Manolo wasn't happy. When the bill arrived Manolo checked it to make sure they hadn't added any extras. Another lesson learned. Because eating out in Cuba is so reasonable, it had never occurred to me to check the bill.

After the meal my amigos began presenting me with gifts. Although I always tell them it isn't necessary to give me gifts, every year they do. When they presented me with wedding gifts to take to Carene, I was very touched. They also had gifts for Anne, as well as Richard and Julie. It was a Cuban/Canadian lovefest.

Adelaida went all out to make our last breakfast special. She had taken a tomato and cut it in wedges, making it look like a flower, and placed a banana in the centre. We were also served pastry and a chocolate filled with crushed nuts and caramel. Everything looked very pretty and I was touched by the trouble she had gone to.

Observations and Reflections - 2011

When things don't come easily to people, and they are given a gift, they have a way of making the most out of it. When the people of Muraleando were given an old water tank, they had a vision to turn it into a cultural centre for Muraleando, and with a lot of hard work they accomplished their goal.

No matter what country you're in, people love a party. All you need is some music, some refreshments and people – put them together and the result is fun.

Two people can visit a humble dwelling in Cuba and see things differently. One person sees sparse living quarters where a family shares a small space and it breaks her heart. Another sees a family whose love for each other is evident and sees a home.

When travelling to another country, especially a country like Cuba, sometimes plans can go awry. The best thing to do is deal with the obstacle like a Cuban would – rethink the situation and carry on.

Bonnie Martin

October 2011

People You'll Meet

Yamelis

Yamelis is the wife of Dr. Rodovaldo in Las Terrazas

Waldo Rodriguez del Rey and his wife Amileidis

The owners of the casa Bella Perla Marina in Cienfuegos

Chapter Fifteen

In 2011 a lot of things had happened in my life – some happy and some sad. My oldest and dearest friend, Marilyn, succumbed to cancer in August, and one month later, my daughter Carene got married. It had all been an emotional whirlwind and I needed some time to reflect. I needed a Cuba fix.

Travel is usually better when it's shared with someone, but for me, there are times I like travelling solo, and this was one of them. I would spend some time in Havana, and then do some travelling with Juan, my guide and friend. I wouldn't have to concern myself with pleasing anyone, and all Juan had to concern himself with was keeping me happy.

I didn't arrive into Havana until late, and even though it was after eleven by the time I cleared customs, I felt fairly comfortable because I had made this trip numerous times. There are always people outside the airport who help co-ordinate taxis, which is very helpful, so in no time I was on my way.

A Moment in Time - Hitchin' a ride

Because I had a taxi to myself, I sat up front with the driver. The road we were travelling on is a winding four-lane that makes its way through Miramar, one of the prettiest parts of Havana.

When we were stopped at a light, I noticed something odd going on beside us. A fellow on a ten-speed bicycle stopped behind one of the old classic cars and knocked on the rear fender, asking for permission to hitch a ride. When it was granted, he turned and motioned to another cyclist to move forward. The first rider leaned over his handle bars and held onto the car's bumper, while the second fellow grasped the back of the first rider's saddle. The light turned green and they all proceeded, while I stared agape. I looked at my driver, who was also watching, and he just shrugged his shoulders.

While I was eating breakfast at Adelaida's, her sister and son came in to greet me. Her son, a musician, extended an invitation to hear him play that evening. He was filling in with a band that was playing in Vedado at a new venue. Adelaida said there was a nice French restaurant across from the bar and suggested Juan and I have dinner there, and then go and hear the band. It all sounded like a good idea, so when Juan came to pick me up we made a plan.

Juan had Lazaro take us to the bus station to purchase our tickets for Las Terrazas and Cienfuegos. With that done, we went to pick up Jesús at his apartment and then we would all go to Muraleando.

Jesús' aunt was ill and in hospital, so he was spending a great deal of time there taking care of her. Because he was sleeping at the hospital every other night, he wanted to go home to shower and change before meeting with us.

Hospital care in Cuba is very different from what we in Canada are used to. They have an excellent and free medical system, but the daily care of patients is the family's responsibility. The year I volunteered, while working at a hospital, I witnessed people carrying in things like food and fans for patients.

Following is an excerpt from a letter I received from Jesús:

> Life continues testing us all the time. Last Wednesday, my Aunt Vita fell to the floor and broke her left hip. To our surprise, she was operated yesterday after lunch. I sleep there at the hospital every other night. The doctors and paramedical people are nice and efficient and it is hard to believe that all that is for free. Food

unfortunately is not very good, but is what they can give. Relatives, who can, bring extra from their homes.

Tomorrow I have to go there again in the evening to spend the night. My aunt is sleeping hours and hours, thanks to God, and does not complain much about pain. She is getting an intravenous and also strong antibiotic in her vein to prevent any infection of the wound. The doctor said her leg cannot touch the floor for three months. What a test.

Her mind is very clear and we speak about mutual memories from my childhood. I always try to make her smile. We will continue our special care of her since she has always been a nice aunt for us. Now she is in need with no means at all. My CUC were coming to an end when I needed some extra money to face this illness of Vita. I looked into my small zipper nylon bag and still had two flash memories that were given to me in August so I was able to sell them.

At Jesús' apartment I was pleasantly surprised to find Victor (the older one) from Muraleando there visiting. He works close by so drops in when he has a break. I had brought pictures from Carene's wedding and as we looked at them Victor said a very nice thing. He told me Carene was beautiful to look at, but her beauty comes from the inside. She is always happy and has a wonderful sense of humour. It certainly was a nice thing to hear.

We went to Muraleando and after visiting with a few of the artists we walked over to El Tanque, and once again I was in awe of what had been accomplished. Windows and a large front door had been installed and the roof had been completed. The inside of the tank was painted a bright aqua, representing the water the tank had once held. Each artist's work hung in individual sections, and there were displays of work done by children at workshops held in Muraleando.

As I was being shown the progress, I was told the roof had leaked, damaging some of the art. They worried that the cost to repair it would be more than they could afford at this time. I had brought a sizable donation that I hadn't yet given them, so I knew it would be put to good use.

Back at Manolo's for lunch, I presented him with donations from Fred and me, Richard and Julie, and Anne. It pleased me to know that they could fix the roof on the tank.

The next day, while touring The Museum of the Revolution, I received a fantastic lesson in Cuban history, reminding me how knowledgeable Jesús is about Cuba, and how good he is at his job. The Museum of the Revolution, located in the former presidential palace, was home to twenty-one Cuban presidents, and finally, the dictator, Batista. It is an absolutely beautiful building, decorated by Tiffany of New York, with more marble than I have ever seen in one place. When we entered, we did have a laugh, witnessing Socialism at its finest. Just inside the door a woman took our entrance fee and in turn gave us a small ticket. A few steps farther was another woman, whose sole job was to take our tickets, tear them, then give them back to us. Jesús commented how stressful her high pressure job must be.

Part of the museum was closed to the public for refurbishing, but there was still a great deal to see. The three of us sat on a bench in a hallway while Jesús gave me a condensed version of early history, beginning when Christopher Columbus first laid eyes on Cuba, and continuing up to when the Revolution began.

We walked through the different rooms filled with documents, photographs and memorabilia, presenting an overview of the Cubans' struggle for independence from the Colonial period on, but focussing in particular on the Revolution. Many of the pictures were difficult to look at, but made it clear that war is a terrible thing, no matter when or where it occurs. Looking at pictures and displays showing clothes and uniforms of the people involved in the Revolution, what came to mind was just how recent this history was, a mere fifty-three years ago.

A Moment in Time - Happy hour with Adelaida

Adelaida's son had recently been married, and since I had brought pictures of Carene's wedding, Adelaida suggested we all sit in her sun room and have a drink while we looked at pictures from both weddings. She brought out a tray with four glasses of amaretto, and a small silver plate of chocolates, then proposed a toast to friends, Canada and Cuba.

Juan and I met at the Lazaros for a visit, and then I was taking everyone out for dinner. While visiting in February, I learned that big brother and his girlfriend were expecting a baby, so when I had the chance, I discreetly gave him some CUC to help prepare for the new arrival. For the rest of the evening, every time he was near me, he would squeeze my arm or shoulder and whisper thank you. It brings me pleasure to be able to help my Cuban friends, knowing a little goes a long way.

We went to a new restaurant, located in a once-abandoned building that had recently been rebuilt. Cuba is in the process of refurbishing many of the old buildings to help attract the tourist dollar. There would be a floor show later with flamenco dancers, so I thought it would make for an enjoyable evening. The food was very good, and the dancers were amazing. We were seated very close to the stage, enabling me to see the energy that goes into flamenco performances. When the dancers asked for audience participation, Melina, her boyfriend, and Lazaro got up. Melina had studied dance for years, including flamenco, so she was keen.

The evening was wonderful, just too short. We said our weepy good-byes until next year.

Chapter Sixteen

I was up early to meet Juan and catch the bus to Las Terrazas. As we were checking into Moka Hotel, the doctor called Juan, excited about our visit, since my last one had been such a disappointment for him. We arranged to meet for dinner, and because I had learned that he now had a new woman in his life, I invited his family to join us.

Juan and I walked to the boat house for lunch and then had our first café at Café Maria. Once again, I thought how fortunate are the people who reside in Las Terrazas.

It had been an early morning, so we both retired to our rooms for a siesta. When I turned on the television to catch some news on CNN, the headlines were that Muammar Gaddafi had been killed. Here I was in paradise, away from it all, but I couldn't escape the horrors going on in other parts of the world. After watching for a few minutes, I decided I'd heard enough. I turned off the television, opened my balcony door then lay down and drifted off while listening to the sounds of nature outside.

We met the doctor at Fonda de Mercedes and were introduced to his wife, Yamelis, as well as her daughter. Throughout the evening, it was obvious that the doctor was in a new relationship. He and Yamelis continually held hands, or he had his arm around her. Oh, to be newly in love!

The doctor told us a band was playing at the disco that evening, so Juan and I thought we'd check it out.

A Moment in Time - A school dance

Arriving at the disco, we realized the music was actually for a school dance, with young people ranging in age from eight to around sixteen in attendance. We didn't seem to be cramping anyone's style, so thought we'd stay for a while and have a beer. Most danced in groups, and every time a new song began, they all squealed. A few of the older students sat in the darker corners smooching. Juan and I even danced a couple of dances.

The dance ended around eleven and we left with everyone else. A light rain was just beginning to fall, and as we walked toward the hotel a young girl behind us began talking to Juan in earnest, telling him that we should walk faster so we wouldn't get wet. When Juan didn't react enough, she added, "Do you know what I'm telling you?" He just smiled and replied that he understood.

We were going on a walking and bird-watching tour, so met up with a guide and two couples from England. Walking along back roads, the guide pointed out different birds, as well as plants. Knowing that Cuban people use plants for a variety of medicinal purposes, I found that part of the tour quite interesting.

At a lookout with a beautiful view of Las Terrazas below, we could hear noise that kept growing louder, and discovered it was coming from a group of school children out for Exploration Day. The guide confronted the children and scolded them, saying they were making so much noise, they were scaring the birds. About fifteen sets of big brown eyes stared at him, not saying a word. When he finished his lecture, he turned and smiled at us, as the children continued on their way. The funny thing was, before long, the noise was back to the same level it had been. I commented that if the same situation happened in Canada, the guide would have been sworn at or worse. My English friends said the same would be true in England.

Yamelis had suggested that before leaving Las Terrazas, we should visit Casa del Campesino, a restaurant located approximately three kilometres from the village. Juan had a little trouble arranging a taxi as one was in for repairs, and the other had gone to Havana, but finally, the hotel desk clerk arranged for a resident to take us in his Jeep.

Casa del Campesino, which translated means house of the peasant, sits on a lovely piece of property, surrounded by lush greenery, and brightly coloured wild flowers. The original house is where the cooking is done, and beside it is a large covered patio. The menu contained the usual Cuban fare and we both opted for chicken. Served farm-style, we received a platter of chicken, slow roasted and in delicious au jus, a large bowl of rice, black beans and banana chips. We both agreed it was the best chicken we'd ever tasted. While we ate, two older gentlemen serenaded the people dining.

We sat a while taking in our surroundings then Juan went into the house asking them to call the hotel to send the taxi to fetch us. That's when things began to go awry. A woman from the house told Juan there was no taxi available to pick us up. We couldn't believe our ears. This was one of those times when I let Juan handle things. That's what I pay him for, and I didn't think he needed me telling him how to handle the situation. He went back to the house, asking them to call the hotel again. The reply came back that they would try to send someone. At that point Juan began to get annoyed. He called the hotel from his cell phone, and I could tell from his tone that he meant business. He asked the desk clerk, "What do you mean there are no taxis? What are we supposed to do, sleep here?" A few minutes later a van arrived to take us back. I don't know how the hotel rounded up the driver, but when I asked him how much I owed him, he told me "Whatever you want." As Juan and I discussed the events of the day, things began to make sense. He said that on the way to the restaurant in the Jeep, the driver had told him he was annoyed when the hotel clerk summoned him to take us because he had just started repairing his vehicle. What I couldn't understand was why the clerk had sent us to the restaurant if he knew we couldn't get back.

Back in the village, we walked around visiting some local artists' galleries and then came upon what I thought was a beautiful sight. Tucked into one of the far corners of the village, behind the daycare centre, four older ladies sat under a palapa playing dominoes. It was quiet, with a gentle breeze, and I thought, what a wonderful way for senior people to spend time. In the welcoming way of the Cuban people, we were asked to sit down. One lady told us she had lived in Las Terrazas all her life, and another said she had married a local man and had been there thirty-five years. A couple of years later, I would learn that we were actually at a senior's daycare centre, where older people can go and spend the day so they aren't left alone while their families are working.

We headed to Café Maria and indulged in a café with chocolate, which Juan loved. Back in my room for siesta, my thoughts were, life doesn't get much better than this.

When we met for dinner, Juan told me the doctor was waiting for us at the desk. What followed was a case of me being clued out, and Juan and the doctor being overly polite. I don't want the doctor to feel obligated to spend time with us because I know how busy he is. We chatted for a while and he told us he would try to see us the next day before we left, then said he would walk with us to the vegetarian restaurant. I was oblivious to the fact he wanted to join us. During dinner I began to figure things out, and when I questioned Juan, I could tell by his expression I was correct. I asked him why he hadn't said something, and he told me he didn't think it was his place to do so. I felt bad, but I would make it up to the doctor at a later time.

We thought we'd go to the hotel bar for a drink and found it busy. A tour group of women from different countries in the British Isles were there, and they were partying. When we had seen them at breakfast and lunch, they were barely talking. It's amazing what good Cuban rum can do. They invited us to join them and we all had a great time for the rest of the evening. It's always fun meeting fellow travellers.

We were leaving Las Terrazas today, so arranged for a taxi to take us to Havana. The doctor wanted to meet us to say good-bye, but since he was on duty, he had to play it by ear. On our way to have our last café, we heard him call to us, saying he could join us. We sat chatting then Juan said he had to leave us briefly to make some calls. Between the doctor's shyness and the language barrier, the conversation was a little difficult but we managed. He told me that his assistant had taken a patient to Pinar del Río, and still hadn't returned, so he had patients waiting.

A woman came to the entrance of the café, trying to get the doctor's attention. She had scalded her leg and wanted advice on how to get some relief. He told her to mix up some egg whites and spread them over the burn. I had never heard of that remedy, but after returning home I looked it up. There were mixed opinions, but in Cuba they have to rely on natural remedies more than we do.

From Café Maria you can look across the way and see the medical clinic, and I noticed the doctor kept looking in that direction. Juan still hadn't returned and I don't think the doctor wanted to leave me at Café Maria alone. It wouldn't have been a problem, but when he asked me if I had time to go to his office with him, I agreed. At the clinic, people sat waiting on the benches outside his office, and when I told him I felt I was keeping him from his work, he assured me it wasn't a problem.

Sitting in with the doctor

Arriving at the doctor's office, it embarrassed me that I was the cause of the people being kept waiting, but they all smiled at me. I did notice a boy of about thirteen, not looking well at all, lying on a bench with his head in his father's lap. We entered the office and the doctor told me to take a seat. By now I was feeling downright uncomfortable.

The first patient was called in - the boy with his concerned looking father. As the doctor spoke to the father, I smiled at the boy, who was pale and very lethargic looking. When the doctor finished speaking with the father, he asked the boy to pull up his pant leg. What I saw was a nasty gash, about two inches long that it had been done by a scythe. It had been stitched but had become infected and was now split open. There was a knock at the door and it was Juan, so now there were five of us in the office, but the boy's father just smiled at us. The doctor explained everything to Juan, who in turn filled me in. The doctor made sure we knew that he hadn't been the one to stitch the wound originally. He took the young man into the examination room to clean the wound and administer a shot of antibiotics. He then gave the father a script for more antibiotics.

The next patient was a little boy of about three with his mother. She told the doctor her son was having a problem with his ear. The boy kept pulling on his ear lobe, but other than that, he seemed happy enough, and was as active as any normal three year old. The doctor asked the mother questions, then, held the boy's head while he smelled his ear, to tell if it was infected. Another knock came to the door and it was the father of the first patient saying the *farmacia* couldn't fill the script he had been given, so another was written. Unfortunately, that sort of thing occurs more often than it should.

Cuba has a first-rate medical system, but a shortage of drugs, partly due to the U.S. embargo. For that reason, before visiting Cuba I ask my doctor for any samples from drug companies that I can take with me. Simple things such as pain relievers are very much appreciated in Cuba.

After the mother and her son left, we told the doctor we should be on our way. He walked us out, thanked me again for the meds I had brought, and apologized for not being able to spend more time with us. I received one of his big bear hugs and was told, every time I visit Cuba, I must visit him. I assured him I would certainly try. I left with my head reeling, trying to absorb everything that had just occurred.

Back in Havana, Juan escorted me to Lincoln's casa, where I would stay for one night. He and his wife met me at the door, welcoming me warmly. The lady of the house, who speaks almost no English, told me, "I love you!" to which I replied, "I love you too!" When Lincoln asked if I would like café, I answered, "Si, por favor." It was very dark, but smooth and rich and just what I needed.

After a siesta, I got ready to meet Jesús, Maria, Jenny, Juan and

Mari, to take them all out for dinner. Later, they walked me back to my casa and we said our good-byes. It would be the last time I would see everyone except Juan on this trip. He and I would be travelling to Cienfuegos the following day.

Chapter Seventeen

Juan and I caught the bus for the four-hour drive to Cienfuegos. We would be staying at a casa, Bella Perla Marina, owned by Waldo and his wife Amileidis. We were met at the bus station by Waldo's nephew, and walked the short distance to Bella Perla Marina. Amileidis met us at the door and invited us into a formal sitting room, decorated very traditionally, with rocking chairs and an abundance of porcelain artifacts. A little later, the nephew appeared with glasses of ice-cold orange juice, and soon after Waldo came in, introducing himself. After chatting for a few minutes, Waldo invited us to go up to the rooftop patio, where we would take our meals, and told us we could go there to relax at any time. The patio was lovely, filled with a multitude of plants, a glider swing, and tables and chairs for dining. The three of us stood taking in the view as Waldo pointed out some landmarks and places of interest. We went back downstairs to see the two rooms they offered, and decide who would stay where. The first room contained an antique brass bed that had once belonged to the mayor of Cienfuegos. Waldo said they referred to the bed as a princess bed, so because I consider myself to be a bit of a princess, I chose that room. After doing the necessary paper work to check in, we struck off to find some lunch and explore a little.

*Cienfuegos is a maritime town with one of the most captivating bays in the Caribbean Sea, earning it the name, "Pearl of the South", in the colonial era. Arranged around the calm natural bay, the city has a superb waterside setting. Geographically, the city is split into two distinct parts: the colonnaded central zone with its elegant Prado and salubrious Parque Martí; and Punta Gorda, a thin knife of land that slices into the southern waters of the bay and contains a clutch of eclectic early 20th century palaces along with some of Cuba's prettiest casas particulares. Cienfuegos earned a UNESCO World Heritage site listing in 2005.

The Paseo del Prado is longer than the one in Havana and just as lovely. I find them to be great places to sit, relax, and people watch. We walked around and found ourselves on the Malecón, with the water beside us. When we heard music coming from a nice-looking large patio, we decided to check it out.

A Sunday Afternoon in Cienfuegos

The hostess told us the band would begin soon, so we found a table and ordered drinks. The patio was lovely with a canopy of trees which afforded a nice mix between sun and shade. I have come to learn that the best times in Cuba can be had on Sunday afternoons. I had experienced a fun-filled Sunday in Viñales the previous February and, as people began arriving, I felt today would be the same.

The band began to play and they were excellent. There were bongos, a flute, maracas and some percussion. As the patio began to fill up, I looked around observing the crowd. We were sitting beside a couple, and the woman kept smiling at us. She and her husband were dancing a lot, and as the afternoon wore on, and the rum began to kick in, he became quite funny. Whenever he acted up, his wife sat down, refusing to dance with him. A man with two women and some children arrived and sat near us. They were all dressed in their finest attire, and the man was one stylin' dude, dressed all in white, right down to his boots, with Cuban heels. It was obvious that he loved to dance, because from the moment they walked in, he began dancing, and what a dancer he was! Juan also loves to dance, so we danced a lot. You can dance right beside your table so you don't have to worry about leaving purses and cameras unattended. When Juan took my camera to go and take some pictures, I was asked to dance by the man sitting beside me. By now, the rum had really kicked in with him, and he began doing some fancy moves, wanting me to do the same. All I could do was laugh, while I tried to tell him my Canadian body just couldn't move like his. His wife smiled, and the people around us were laughing. In front of the band, an older gentleman was dancing by himself and, although he was on in years, he still had the moves. I was having the time of my life! After an afternoon like I had just had, I know why I love Cuba so much.

A Moment in Time - The ultimate café for 25¢

Since I began travelling to Cuba, I have become accustomed to enjoying a café in the afternoon. After partying, Juan and I went looking for our afternoon fix. He found a place with a few tables and we ordered espresso. Served in small plastic cups with a straw for stirring, it was the best espresso I'd ever tasted.

We had ordered dinner for seven-thirty so back at the casa I freshened up and relaxed a little. The table on the roof was set, and there was even a small stereo sitting on a chair, so we had music to dine by. It had been a long day, and after my fun-filled afternoon, I was running out of steam, so I told Juan I was going to have an early night. It was lights out for me by ten-thirty and I slept like a baby in my princess bed.

Cienfuegos has many old, beautiful buildings. A prominent one is a theatre, built for a successful businessman, Thomas Terry, who began by buying slaves that had become ill on the voyage from Africa. He would nurse them back to health, and then sell them for a small profit. Later, he built a railroad and ended up amassing a lot of money. On the town square, alongside a statue of José Martí, was a huge ceiba tree, and Juan explained the tree's history. Originally, sailors, before going to sea, would walk around the tree three times and leave coconuts, pumpkins and fruits for good luck. This is done every year on November 16 to commemorate the date of the first mass in Havana. In Havana, people wait for hours to leave gifts, as well as touch and circle the ceiba tree located there.

We entered a cultural centre that, like many buildings in Cuba, was under repairs. A woman was sitting at a table, writing, and Juan began talking with her. We learned she runs a dance company and that some of her students had won awards. She said she used to teach traditional dance, but finds that now everyone wants to dance salsa. A book containing a list of her students, ranging in age from twelve to sixty-nine, numbered over three-hundred.

We walked to the dock to catch a ferry that would take us to a Castillo. Waldo had suggested we go there, telling us that from the Castillo we would be able to see the partially built nuclear power plant near the town of Juragua.

While we waited for the ferry, an enterprising woman came to the dock carrying a large plastic bucket containing small plastic cups of homemade chocolate ice cream that she was selling for fifty Cuban pesos. After selling them all, she walked a short distance to a house and returned with another bucketful.

On the ferry, we rode below deck, on benches, near the bow. The benches filled rapidly, leaving many people either standing or sitting on the floor. With only a few small windows open, and not much ventilation, I wasn't finding the ride very pleasant. The ferry was slow moving, so I was happy when we finally reached our destination. While speaking with a woman on the boat, Juan learned that, as an alternative, we could take a bus back to Cienfuegos.

We were in a small fishing village where the people lived simply. As we walked toward the Castillo, a woman approached, asking if we would be interested in going to her home for lunch after our tour. She said we could dine right beside the water and offered chicken, pork, fish or lobster, with rice and salad for 10 CUC. The price wasn't particularly cheap, but I could tell they had very little, so I didn't mind helping her out.

At the Castillo, a young woman was waiting to also take the tour. The cost was only 1 CUC, and the tour was quite short, which suited me fine. In my travels I've been to a few Castillos and forts and find them to be pretty much alike, no matter what country they are in. It really wasn't worth the time and effort to get there, but I chalked it up to another unique Cuban experience.

Juragua Nuclear Power Plant

From the Castillo we could see the site of the Juragua Nuclear Power Plant and some of the housing that would first house workers building the plant, and later people who would run it. There had been employment for three thousand people when the construction began, which was a great boom to the area. The plan was to build two, 440 megawatt reactors. Construction began in 1983 on the first reactor, and in 1985 on the second. Upon completion, the first reactor would be capable of generating fifteen per cent of Cuba's energy demands, saving two million tons of oil a year. When the accident at the Chernobyl nuclear plant in the Soviet Union occurred in 1986, the people of Cuba became frightened of nuclear power. In 1992, after the collapse of the Soviet Union, construction ceased. A lot of money was wasted in building materials, and one billion dollars was spent in the construction of the first reactor. It would take billions more to complete the plant.

Most of the housing is now abandoned, and the reactor sits visible as a grim reminder of a failed project that would have no doubt had a positive effect on, not only employment, but Cuba's energy needs. It is a topic of conversation in the area, and most are happy it was stopped. When engineers went to inspect the plant they told the Cuban people the work had not been done properly and, if the reactor had been started, they would all be dead. I'm sure some of the story has been embellished, but it probably makes the failure of the project a little easier to take.

I asked Paola, the young woman who had taken the tour of the Castillo with us, to join us for lunch. She was in Cuba hoping to do her thesis, but the Cuban government wouldn't allow her to. It seemed they didn't want her asking officials a lot of questions about how the country is run.

We found the house where we would have our lunch and were directed to a table right beside the water. It was quite pleasant sitting there giving me a chance to see what life is like for people living in small fishing villages in Cuba. When I asked to use the baño, the woman took me up to her house where I witnessed some rather rustic living conditions. The baño was in the bedroom and contained a toilet that didn't flush and a sink with no running water, however, the bed was neatly made and the dresser was decorated with empty perfume bottles.

We took our time with our lunch and sat chatting about our lives. A short ferry ride took us to where we could catch a bus that would take us back to Cienfuegos.

A Moment in Time - An afternoon commute in Cuba

The bus was old, with a lot of seats that were torn and missing big chunks of foam. We sat at the front, behind the driver, so I was able to watch the comings and goings. The bus was empty when we boarded except for a few young school children on their way home. It made frequent stops and began filling up with people, some on their way home from work, and others just finishing their day. Many people greeted the driver in the normal Cuban way, either with a kiss or a handshake. I noticed not everyone paid the fare. As the bus travelled through a few small villages, people got on carrying an array of things. One man boarded with two huge sacks containing cans, and some people carried plastic bags that held fish, perhaps for their evening meal. When a young mother got on carrying her little boy, Juan offered her his seat. The young boy was grasping a crust of bread and never made a sound, just looked around in wonderment with big brown eyes. The ride took about an hour but I loved every minute. I not only got to witness Cuban people going about their everyday lives, but also saw a part of the countryside most tourists wouldn't.

Back in Cienfuegos, we said good-bye to Paola and then walked to the same café we had been at yesterday for another of their excellent espressos.

By the time we arrived back at our casa, I was beginning to feel a little sluggish, and thought perhaps I had over-done things. I had drunk mojitos, probably made with regular ice, and eaten homemade ice cream as well as salad. I wasn't ill, but wanted to be cautious, so as not to spoil the rest of my trip. I went to my room to lie down briefly, then showered and got ready for dinner. I told Juan I wouldn't be going out later, and after another delightful meal, I said goodnight. I went to bed at eight-thirty and slept right through the night, which was probably the best thing I could have done.

Today we would be travelling to Trinidad, a place in Cuba I had always wanted to visit. Waldo arranged a taxi for us, and as we said our good-byes he presented me with a gift, a CD of Cuban music. He told me I reminded him of an aunt he loves, saying I had the same colouring as she does and I was sweet like she is. I thanked him for the CD, the compliment, and the nice stay.

The ride to Trinidad was on back roads with no traffic, making it enjoyable. I saw a cow being butchered in a field and farmers herding animals along the road. At one point we almost hit a dog that crossed in front of us, and later had to dodge a herd of goats. It was after these two close calls that Juan told the driver we weren't in a big hurry to reach Trinidad, and asked him to slow down.

The owners of the casa in Trinidad, a mother and daughter, were friends of Jesús, so he had arranged our stay. When we arrived, we were told there had been a mix-up, and that they were expecting us the previous day. They had spoken with Jesús, who told them when we were arriving, so they made arrangements for us at a casa next door. We were offered café, and as we sat visiting, the younger woman began paying me compliments. She told me I was very elegant, and went on to say she loved the colour of my hair and that my blue eyes were the colour of her grandfather's. I've been called many things in my life, but elegant was never one of them. I thanked her for the compliment.

We went next door to the casa where we would stay and met the owners, a young couple with a little girl about three years old. The casa was a very old, long and narrow house with a court yard behind. Down one side of the court yard was a second kitchen, as well as a room where Juan would stay.

A Moment in Time - The little girl and the chicken

Most Cubans in small towns have chickens in their yard, but the little girl from our casa had a baby chicken for a pet. Her father had fashioned an oval-shaped cage out of chicken wire, and the chicken sat in the bottom with a bowl of feed, while the little girl dragged it around. I have to say, I was feeling a little sorry for the poor chicken as it didn't seem to be enjoying itself one bit. The next day the chicken was running loose, and when the girl's parents told her to round it up so she could play, the chicken was having no part of it. It ran around dodging the girl, hiding under rocking chairs on the patio. The family dog, a small and gentle part dachshund, just hid under Juan's rocking chair keeping out of the way.

Trinidad, population 38,000 was founded in 1514 by Diego Velasquez on a site that had been settled by the Taino Indians. It is a quaint city with cobblestone streets and, like Cienfuegos, seemed to have more horse-drawn carts than cars. In the heart of the city, the main square, Plaza Mayor, is surrounded by old colonial buildings and manicured greenery. A mansion where the owner of a sugar plantation from the area once lived is now a museum. We took a tour, conducted by a very nice woman, who explained the architecture of the house. The walls, around the thick hand-carved doors, and arches in the house were all painted in fresco, making them quite lovely.

When we arrived back at the casa later, the woman and her little girl were standing at the front door and seemed to be waiting for us. Both were dressed up, with the little girl wearing a crisp cotton dress with hair ribbons to match, looking too cute for words. We were told they usually cook for guests, but tonight were attending a birthday celebration. They gave Juan the keys to the house and recommended a paladar for dinner.

We were relaxing in the garden when someone began knocking at the front door in earnest. The house had no windows facing the street, so whoever was knocking couldn't see us. They didn't seem to be giving up, and when I questioned Juan whether we should answer it, he told me that the owner had told him not to. He said that the owners have a young woman who cleans for them, and they are supposed to pay the state a small fee to be used as a type of pension for the worker. Because they weren't paying the fee, the authorities were after it.

In Cuba they have inspectors for just about everything, so my feeling is, it's best to follow the rules. I don't think they are put in place to oppress, but rather to stop people from taking advantage of the system and draining the state. I have been witness to inspectors checking up on casa owners, making sure all the rooms they are renting out are legal. There are inspectors who visit each and every house in Cuba to make sure no one has standing water around where mosquitos might breed. One type of mosquito in Cuba can be very dangerous, spreading Dengue Fever. The funny thing was, Juan and I had noticed some standing water in the courtyard of this casa, so perhaps the owners don't like rules. A lot of people dislike a socialist government, and all the rules and regulations that go along with it, but I'm less concerned with restrictions on my freedom, and would rather have rules in place to protect me from unscrupulous people.

Breakfast was prepared by the man of the house and served in the garden. There was juice, an omelet, bread, fruit and café, and if that wasn't enough, a basket containing two soft rolls, with ham and cheese was also on the table. It was more than I could possibly have eaten, but was all very good. We would be taking the bus back to Havana later, but still had some time to explore so our host arranged a taxi for us.

*The Valley de los Ingenios derives its name from the sugar mills that were built there in the early nineteenth century. The valley is rich in history, with ruins providing evidence of the time when the sugar industry was at its peak. The buildings also help visitors understand the social structure that was the order of the sugar plantations. UNESCO has declared the valley a World Heritage Site.

From a lookout above the valley we could see for miles. At the site, there was a café, a potter working with a small wheel, and people selling different artifacts. Some ladies were selling handmade tablecloths, which seem to be popular items. They were beautiful, made of white cotton, with either hand-embroidered cut work, or done with crocheted cotton trims.

*The Manaca Iznaga Estate is where about three hundred and fifty slaves lived in the 1840s. The landowner's house survives and has been converted into a bar and restaurant. The slaves' huts are still standing, as well as a monumental seven-level, forty-five metre high tower that functioned as a lookout for supervising the slaves. If a slave was caught trying to escape, one of his ears would be cut off as punishment.

Out behind the house and down some stairs was a spot set up for a traditional Cuban party. Chairs formed a large circle around an original mill, used for squeezing sugar cane to extract the juice. Two men tended a fire, working to get it to burn slowly, to roast the pigs. I could see two little porkers on a spit leaning against a tree and thought someone was certainly in store for a feast later. An older woman on the other side of a fence held up a bunch of bananas, trying to get Juan's attention. He purchased them for 25 Cuban pesos, and we both ate one. In Canada, we are so used to bananas that have been picked green, and then pumped full of gas to ripen them, I had forgotten what a fresh banana tastes like.

Still exploring the grounds, we were approached by a young man carrying some sugar cane. He handed us each a large bug made from sugar cane, called an *esperanza,* telling us the name of the bug means "hope". He then placed a handmade bracelet, made out of dried sugar cane with some coloured cane woven in on our wrists. It was a bit of a hard sell, but when Juan asked him how much they were, he replied, "Whatever you want to give me."

When we went to find our waiting taxi, we heard, "Amigos!" It was the woman who had given us the tour of the museum yesterday. She had taken a group of school children to the site to teach them some history of the sugar trade and asked if she could get a ride back to town with us. I found it odd that she would be left to find her own way back, but came to the conclusion that it is a common occurrence for Cubans to help each other out with rides, so no one is truly stranded.

We had some time before our bus so while I did some writing Juan went to visit the two ladies where we were originally supposed to stay. Our hosts had gone out, but the cleaning lady was there, scrubbing the cement in the courtyard. Because the people had chickens, cleaning the cement was necessary. They don't have garden hoses or power washers like we do, so the task was being done by hand.

The family arrived home and the man gave Juan and me a piece of his father's birthday cake, and it was heavenly. In Trinidad, as well as Cienfuegos, cakes are sold on the street, either by the slice or whole. After tasting this one, I wished I had purchased some.

Taking five hours, the bus ride to Havana was longer than I had anticipated, but Juan and I had some nice conversations about our lives and the different customs in each of our countries.

It was raining when we arrived into Havana so many people wanted taxis. We managed to get an unmarked one, driven by a very nice young man. When Juan commented that he liked his car, the driver said he rented it for 15 CUC a day, and mainly hung out near the bus or train stations for fares. He said he had three young children to feed, and this was a way to help do that.

For my last night in Cuba, I was staying at 21 & O with Adelaida. Juan accompanied me upstairs to make sure I would be okay getting to the airport in the morning. My plan was to go across the street where a number of taxis always sit, and get one there but he was concerned that since it would still be dark when I had to leave that I might have trouble so he asked Adelaida if she could arrange a ride for me. I was touched at how well my friend looks after me.

I was up at six o'clock and sat down to a wonderful breakfast. Adelaida told me she had made arrangements with a woman with a private car, and she would come upstairs for me. As we drove to the airport, the city was quite busy with the morning rush hour, and the driver drove very fast, as most do in Cuba. They also drive aggressively, but I find there is no road rage. Driving seems to be like a game, with the rules being "may the best man win".

More Observations and Reflections - 2011

Cuban people are deep feeling, not afraid to show their emotions, and don't have a problem voicing their feelings. Consequently, I've received some compliments, which are always nice to hear.

All over Cuba, especially in the country, many homes and buildings are painted white with blue trim. I don't know if the colours are taken from the Cuban flag, but they are certainly pleasing to the eye.

Section Six

April 2012

Chapter Eighteen

Carene and I were happy to be making another trip to Cuba together since she had missed travelling there in 2011. We were going to spend a few days at the Hotel Nacional where we stayed on three previous visits. We had moved to casas because they were much more economical, but missed staying at the hotel. After checking in, we continued our tradition of going out back for mojitos. It's a wonderful way to begin our vacation.

After breakfast, we met Jesús and Juan in the hotel lobby to make some plans. This day we would be going to Muraleando, so Jesús had Lazaro waiting to drive us. Arriving in Muraleando, we were met with greetings from everyone, with Carene receiving extra hugs and congratulations on her marriage. It was the last day of Muraleando's annual festival so, some events were planned. Debbie, the artist from Winnipeg who visits every year during the festival, was conducting a workshop, and later there would be a concert at El Tanque.

Lunch had been arranged for Debbie, Carene and me, and a table was set up in El Tanque. Mayra had prepared everything at her house and it was brought over. As always, the meal was delicious, and we had a chance to catch up with Debbie.

The bands began arriving and setting up for the concert. One was a group of young people from the area, called Backspace, that Manolo had auditioned and they were making their debut.

At the end of Muraleando's festivals, gifts are presented to the people who help out in different ways as a reward for all of their hard work. I always include toiletries with my gifts, so I was pleased when I saw they had been distributed in the gift bags. A presentation was made to Debbie thanking her for her continued support, and I was given some gifts and thanked for my contributions to the project. Our day in Muraleando had been a lot of fun, albeit too short.

The next would be a leisurely day with Juan. Because we had promised cigars for some family, the cigar factory was our first stop. Havana has many places where you can purchase cigars, but for the freshest product, the cigar factory is the best place to buy them. We walked into Habana Vieja, and when we came upon the Chocolate Museum, I told Juan and Carene we had to go in and have a cold chocolate drink. They had never had the experience, and to me it is a special treat.

We had plans to visit the Lazaros later to see Yonmay's new baby. When we arrived, we stopped at Grandma's apartment, where Yonmay, his partner and the new baby live. In Havana, there is a housing shortage, making it necessary for family to live together much of the time. Grandma's small living room now contained a crib, placed in the corner, next to the TV, with all of the supplies for the baby neatly placed around the outer edges. A lot of people in Canada have cribs that meet safety standards, change tables that match the crib, and highly decorated baby nurseries. We make sure things are quiet for the little one, and even have baby monitors so we can listen to the baby from another part of the house. When I saw how they had made room for their new arrival, it put things into perspective. The baby was being fed so we would see him and Mom upstairs a little later.

The rest of the family was waiting for us, and after greetings, we settled in for a visit. Melina had become a beautiful young woman and was studying modelling. She put on a pair of heels and gave us a demonstration of her perfected model's walk. When the new parents arrived with the baby, dressed in his finery, Carene and I presented gifts we had brought for him. We gave gifts to the rest of the family and then Mariela presented both Carene and me with handmade wooden boxes, which touched us both.

After three nights at the Hotel Nacional, we were going to Varadero for a couple of days at an all-inclusive resort. In all the years that Carene had accompanied me to Cuba, she had never spent any time at a beach there. I booked the same resort where I had spent a day in 2006 with The View. Two nights at the resort, including bus fare from Havana and back cost only 200 CUC, so it was a good side trip at a reasonable cost. The resort rated 4½ stars, so there were a few things lacking, but it was clean, and for two nights we could make do. The resorts in Cuba are rated higher than they would be in another country. The weather didn't co-operate fully, but we did manage to get in some beach time, and the trip gave us a chance to catch up on life, so was well worth it.

Back in Havana, we were staying with Adelaida for one night, and then travelling to Las Terrazas for a couple of days.

Rather than taking the bus, we arranged to have Lazaro drive us. Upon arrival we went to the bar for a drink to give Lazaro a bit of a break before he headed back to Havana. He had never been to Las Terrazas before, and as Juan explained the surroundings to him, I could tell he was in awe.

One of the things I look forward to in Las Terrazas is café at Café de Maria. There is no place on earth where I would rather drink café, so after lunch that is where we headed.

We checked into our room, and Juan was pleased that he would be staying with Barbara in community housing. He had stayed with her on two previous visits so it felt like home to him. Barbara told him that the doctor and his family were on vacation, so we wouldn't be seeing him. I was a little disappointed because, not only do I love seeing him, but I had brought some gifts for him and his family, as well as a donation to help him fix his computer, which he had been having problems with. I left everything with Barbara, and she would make sure he got it. After returning home, I received a lovely note from the doctor thanking me.

Carene and I had brought a bottle of rum with us, so after a walk, Juan came to our room for some drinks. I find he relaxes a little more when I'm not paying for drinks, which I don't mind doing, but I do like to see him relax.

For dinner, we went to El Romero, the vegetarian restaurant, and ordered an array of dishes to share. Carene and I both had a drink made with rum, fresh orange juice and fresh ginger which was excellent. Dessert was orange mouse, served in a scooped out orange half. It was so good, it made me think I'd died and gone to heaven.

The next day we went for a walk around Las Terrazas and then to

Barbara's for café. While we visited, Juan told her that I was trying to learn *Español,* and she came up with a suggestion. She said, "You come to Cuba for fifteen days and stay with me. We will speak only Spanish, I'll do all your laundry, and I'll teach you how to cook Cuban." It certainly sounded like something I would like to do, and told her I would consider it. As much as I loved the idea, I wasn't sure if I could spend two weeks in Las Terrazas alone, but when I discussed the idea with Juan later, he told me he would stay there with me. I had something to think about when I returned home.

We thought we'd go to the Río San Juan for the afternoon, so Juan arranged for a taxi. Many cats and dogs live around the river, so when you are in the restaurant, cats will come around looking for food. On this particular day we were visited by a little black kitten that Carene began to feed. She named her Juanita, after Juan and the Río San Juan, which seemed quite fitting. Later we found a nice spot, and as I sat dangling my feet in the water, Carene and Juan had a long swim.

A Moment in Time – Juan gets gypped

As we were leaving the river, an older gentleman approached Juan, showing him a basket of fruit he was selling. The basket was handmade out of palm bark, and filled with mangos and other fruit. He was selling everything, basket and all for 1 CUC, so Juan bought it. After the man left, Juan was checking out his purchase and he wasn't very pleased. The mangos on the top were okay, but the fruit underneath was terrible. Poor Juan was so put out that he left the whole thing sitting on the table.

Our time in Las Terrazas was coming to an end, too quickly for me, but I knew I would be back. We had a taxi ordered for one-thirty to take us back to Havana, so we stowed our bags and went for one last walk. I soon learned it wasn't going to be a peaceful one, because I wasn't walking fast enough to suit Carene. After two days of walking up and down the many stairs in Las Terrazas, my legs were feeling it.

I told her to belt up while reminding her that I had a few years on her, and after all, we were on vacation. We had our last lunch of fish at the boat house, sitting in the sunshine, beside the water. I was missing Las Terrazas already, and I hadn't even left.

When we arrived back in Havana, Carene didn't want our holiday to end, so suggested we all go to the Hotel Nacional for some drinks. It was a gorgeous day and as we sat on the rock, sipping mojitos and looking out over the blue water, once again I was feeling sad to be leaving Cuba.

We noticed a Santería priestess standing on the Malecón looking out to sea. Juan explained she was probably offering prayers to her Orisha, Yemaya, who is the goddess of the sea, and the mother of Orishas. I don't understand much about Santería, but as I sat watching her offer her prayers, I thought what I was looking at was a beautiful sight

Observations and Reflections – 2012

I realized in writing this book that I use the word delicious a lot when I'm talking about food in Cuba. One of the things said frequently about Cuba is, you don't go for the food. I'm afraid that I couldn't disagree more. The problem most people, especially Canadians, have with the food is they mainly go to all-inclusive resorts. While the food at resorts isn't bad, you can't compare it to Cuban home cooking.

This world we live in has many beautiful places, and I am lucky enough to live in one of them - Canada. When I first visited Las Terrazas, I was stunned by the beauty there. Every time I visit, I discover more that I love about it. I now think of Las Terrazas as my favourite place on earth to be.

Section Seven

April 2013

Chapter Nineteen

This would be Carene's and my fifth trip to Cuba together and this time we were changing things up a little. Because their times and fares worked better for us, we flew with WestJet, which meant flying into Varadero. Juan picked us up in a taxi, which was one of the old cars, driven by a fellow by the name of Frank. Even with a 70 CUC charge for the two-hour drive to Havana, I was still saving money.

I wanted this trip to be a little more luxurious so we were staying at one of Havana's better hotels, the Hotel Parque Central. Comparing it to the Hotel Nacional, everything seemed to be just one step up. While the Hotel Nacional and their grounds are beautiful, they do rely a lot on the hotel's history as a selling point.

When we arrived we were hungry and thirsty, and since our room wasn't ready, we sat in the lobby restaurant/bar and ordered mojitos and a sandwich. Juan called Jesús who said he would come and see us so we could make plans for the evening. It was decided we would all go out for dinner, and then to a ball game.

We went to a new restaurant, called Mango Habana, which was an excellent choice, with good food and lots of it. Some of the rules in Cuba have changed in the last few years, one being free enterprise is now allowed, so there has been a positive change in the restaurant scene.

During dinner Jesús excused himself to make a phone call to arrange for a driver to take us to the ball game. Our driver arrived, dressed in his ball shirt and ball cap and I was pleasantly surprised when I saw that it was Carlos. He had been a driver for us in 2009, but I hadn't seen him since then. At the stadium Juan was told that the woman who worked the window for tourists had left, so Carene and I paid the Cuban price, 1 Cuban peso, which equalled about 20¢. The game was exciting, with the Havana team winning 2 – 1 in the bottom of the tenth inning. A baseball game is something everyone who visits Cuba should experience at least once.

We were up early after a comfortable first night, and went down for the included breakfast which was quite impressive. The choice of the Parque Central hotel was proving to be a good one.

Juan and Jesús picked us up and we went to the Museum of the Revolution. I had been there before and found it so interesting that I wanted Carene to experience it. When we left the museum, it was very hot and humid, so I suggested we all go to the Chocolate Museum for a cold chocolate drink. Jesús was the only one in the group who hadn't experienced the drink, and somehow I knew he would like it. After he had taken his first sip, I knew I was right. Jesús is very enthusiastic and quite hyper, so consequently drinks quickly. As he raved about the drink, saying he had to bring Jenny there for one, he was slurping away, so before long he was finished. When I suggested we order two more and share, I certainly didn't have to twist his arm.

We were going to Muraleando, so after lunch Carene and I went back to the hotel to get ready for our visit. It was the middle of Muraleando's 2013 festival and we were invited to share in the day's festivities. My friend Debbie, the artist from Winnipeg, had been there for a few weeks conducting workshops for children and adults, so we would have the chance to see her.

One of the things Muraleando has begun doing to raise money is offer group tours of the project. The groups arrive by bus, are given a walking tour, then treated to some music and dancing at El Tanque. Depending on the tour, they sometimes stay for a meal, made by women from Muraleando.

Victor gave us a tour so we could see the progress made on El Tanque. They had finished the roof, and it was now a beautifully tiled dance floor for future parties. A bar had been installed and there was a lookout with a stunning view of Havana. On a lower level was a bathroom with a shower, and a bunkie that enabled them to offer accommodation for visiting artists. The kitchen now had running water, which seemed to thrill them the most.

It began to rain, and soon was pouring, so we all gathered under cover, huddling in chairs set up for the expected tour. The rain turned into a torrent like I had never seen. Water ran down the stairs, and as we sat trying to wait it out, we had to shout to be heard over the sound of the rain falling on the metal roof.

Since all of the work had stopped, I took the opportunity to present a card to Manolo with a donation for Muraleando, and it turned out to be quite a moment. I had given donations to Muraleando before, but never one this size. As everyone watched, Manolo read the card and then began counting the money out loud. It was plain to see he was thrilled with the donation, and I was thrilled to be able to give it to them.

During the frenzy of activity, an incident occurred that showed me once again how Cuban people won't let an obstacle get the better of them. As it poured, various artists were outside trying to keep the water at bay. Above the din of the rain, we heard a thud and felt the ground shiver ever so slightly. Someone came in and began speaking with Manolo, and judging by the look on his face, it didn't look good. A brick wall they had recently built had collapsed, and now lay spread across the sidewalk. I felt bad for everyone, especially Manolo. He had been so happy mere moments ago, and now this. He only let what had happened get him down for a few minutes, then realizing there was nothing that could be done about it right then, he continued being the gracious host he always is.

The rain finally let up, and before long the bus tour arrived. They were older people from different parts of the USA and quite interested in learning about Muraleando. A tour was given of the project and then they were taken to El Tanque to view the art on display. Later, while they watched a short musical review by some of the artists and children, tables and chairs were set up and food that had been prepared at Manolo's home was transported over. We were all invited to take seats and enjoyed a marvelous meal.

We said good night, wishing everyone well. At the hotel, over a nightcap in the lobby bar, we talked about the wonderful time we had experienced yet again in Muraleando.

On a day of relaxation we wouldn't be seeing Jesús or Juan. We slept in, and after a leisurely breakfast went to purchase our rum and coffee. I got a little carried away, purchasing fifteen two-pound bags, which sent the sales clerk into shock. Now all I had to do was figure out how to get it home. We spent a wonderful afternoon at the pool, sitting in the sun and drinking mojitos, while listening to great music from a live band. For dinner we thought we'd return to Mango Habana, where we had been on our first night. A perfect day was ended with drinks on the roof of the Hotel Inglaterra.

There was going to be a concert in Vedado which Jesús thought we would like. Because it would be a popular event, Carlos drove us to Vedado to purchase our tickets ahead of time. The price for Carene and me was 20 CUC, while Jesús and Juan's was 1 CUC. The arts are so important in Cuba the state tries to make every aspect of them affordable.

When we were picked up for the concert, Carlos greeted us looking very dapper, and we learned he was also attending the concert. It was obviously a dressy affair, so I was glad we had dressed up. When we got to the door of the concert hall, I realized I didn't have Carene's and my tickets. I had changed purses and left the tickets at the hotel. My stomach went into a knot and my heart sank. I was ready to purchase two new tickets, but I needn't have worried. Juan and Jesús took over, speaking with the woman at the gate and explaining our problem. Our tickets were easily traced, and after things were straightened out, the woman left the gate and escorted us to our seats. I was very impressed.

The theatre was beautiful and as nice as any large theatre I had ever been in. The headliner, referred to as the Cuban Bob Dylan, and backed up by a full band, did a few numbers then introduced a number of guests. The concert was very enjoyable and well done.

A Moment in Time - A nightcap at the Parque Central

After the concert, Juan joined Carene and me for a nightcap. In the lobby bar, we watched as a woman sold brandy and cigars from a fancy bar cart. When a cigar was purchased, it would be lit by the woman. She would light the tip and then alternate blowing on the lit tip and using a hand held fan to agitate the air. When the cigar was burning just right, it would be passed to the gentleman.

Chapter Twenty

For our travel to Las Terrazas, Juan drove us in a small car he had rented. With free enterprise now being allowed in Cuba, people who own cars will rent them out to guides, enabling them to better accommodate their clients. It is a good way for the car owner to make some money, and a more convenient way of travelling while in Cuba.

In Las Terrazas, it seemed we were expected which made us feel very special. The woman at the desk told Juan that she had instructions to call the doctor the moment we arrived, and the parking lot attendant, who we learned was Yamelis' father, also let him know we had arrived. Juan spoke with the doctor by phone and was told that he had made reservations for us at Casa del Campesino for three o'clock. After stowing our bags, it was time to visit Café Maria. It's after my first café there that I feel like I'm actually where I belong.

When we met the doctor in the lobby, he was alone. I questioned Juan as to why his wife wasn't joining us for lunch and he said that even though he had made it clear that she was invited, the doctor wasn't sure and didn't want to over step.

At lunch, the doctor told us he wanted to show us a camp in the area where Cuban people can go for a holiday. These camps are a common way for people to get out of the city for a holiday. They are transported there by bus and can rent equipment they will need at a reasonable cost. The camp had a large open space with a hard-surfaced area that acted as a court for various games, and doubled as a dance floor. Off to one side was a large restaurant to buy reasonably priced meals with Cuban pesos, and another smaller one for tourists, who pay in CUC. The camp seemed pretty empty, but there was music blaring. I thought perhaps the people would rather listen to nature and quiet but I'm not Cuban, so what do I know? The property was dotted with small cabins, and when the doctor approached one that was occupied, asking if he could show it to us, the family agreed. Inside were some crude bunk beds, a toilet and sink, and a small hot plate that I assumed was for warming baby food or to make café. The family was sitting on the beds, watching a flat screen TV mounted on the wall. I found it odd that they were inside watching TV, but then remembered being in a home where the only TV was a small black and white with rabbit ears, so maybe to this family watching a nice TV was a treat. Not far from the camp was a spot on the Río San Juan where the people could swim.

As our holiday progressed, we found that we could hear music coming from the camp at all hours of the day and night. One morning Carene rose very early and thought she would have a leisurely bath while watching the sun come up. She said it was all very blissful until, around six-thirty, the music began again and the quiet came to a screeching halt.

In the winter, I had fallen and sprained my arm and was still experiencing some pain and swelling. I thought the good doctor could help me, using the form of Chinese medicine he practices, so I made arrangements for him to treat me while I was in Las Terrazas. After our lunch together, he came to my room and gave me my first treatment, after which we arranged to meet him and his wife later for drinks.

Carene, Juan and I relaxed in our room with some rum, and as the rum disappeared, two things happened. Juan became quite funny, making us laugh, but when he began to talk about his love for Cuba, and how well he believes the people are treated, he became a little emotional. By the time we met the doctor and his wife, we were all feeling the effects of the rum, and because we had been relaxing for so long, were also looking a bit disheveled. I was a little embarrassed because they had obviously dressed for the occasion, both looking as fresh as daisies. While we visited, I told the doctor and Yamelis that I was thinking of visiting Las Terrazas in October to practice my Spanish. Yamelis told me she would also help me, and since she was trying to master English, I could return the favour and help her. The more I talked about my plan, the more excited I became.

Having a car at our disposal, gave us the freedom to do some touring in the area. We went to Soroa to view the waterfall, and later visited a botanical garden.

*Soroa

Very close to Las Terrazas, and in the middle of the same tropical forest, is the small village of Soroa. It was named after two brothers, who in the mid-1800s, bought various coffee plantations and soon became the proprietors of the entire territory.

Today, Soroa is a small holiday village with a few tourist attractions, one being a spectacular waterfall on the Manantiales River. To reach the waterfall you must walk down approximately two hundred steps that wind their way to many places where people can picnic, swim, or just take in the beauty. Like the Río San Juan, the park is well maintained by men who tend the grounds, as well as watch over the cars in the parking lot. The park has an outdoor restaurant as well as a canteen, and the cost to use the facility is a reasonable 2 CUC.

A Moment in Time - Taking pride in one's work

After walking down the many stairs to view the waterfall, I sat on a rock with my feet in the water and watched a man who was busy tending the grounds, sweeping the earth with a handmade broom, while picking up dead leaves and the odd piece of garbage. He worked away on a small area of ground making it picture perfect. When he finished his work, he washed up in the river, then sat in a chair and relaxed. Watching him made me wonder who leads a better life – him, probably not making much money, but working in peaceful surroundings at his own pace, or we in North America, dealing with the rat race every day so we can buy many possessions that we don't really need.

After my profound thoughts, it was time to view some beautiful orchids. Very close to Soroa is a botanical garden called Orquideario, which has been declared a national monument. It was founded in 1943 by a lawyer from the Canary Islands, who had orchids sent there from all over the world in memory of his daughter who had died in childbirth. The site was stunning with stone walkways and steps, all leading to the many gardens.

Juan asked us if we would like to have lunch at *Castillo de las Nubes*, which translated means, Castle in the Clouds. After driving up a very steep hill, we reached the castle, now containing a small restaurant. Beside the restaurant, a swimming pool, situated on the edge of a cliff, enables people to swim while taking in the panoramic view.

That night for dinner, we went again to El Romero, the vegetarian restaurant. I know Juan loves it there because it is different from the food he usually eats. We were told they had a new cook, and asked if we would write comments in their book after our meal. We all wrote positive remarks and Carene noticed the staff in the kitchen patting the cook on the back, and her smiling. After dinner, at the hotel bar, we learned they were offering a new cocktail called *Mira de Las Terrazas*. It was very good and has become a favourite summertime drink at home.

Mira de Las Terrazas Cocktail

- Slice a lime then cut the slices into very small triangles
- Muddle the limes in an old fashioned glass with sugar
- Add white rum and a touch of Triple Sec
- Fill the glass with ice and sparkling water

Today was going to be a day of relaxation at the hotel pool. It was my first time using it, and I was impressed with what was offered. There was a nice eating area under cover or, if you preferred, umbrella tables and lounge chairs around the pool.

A Moment in Time - Not sweating the small stuff

A Cuban family had eaten their lunch around the pool. When they were back in the water, their leftovers became fair game for the many chickens roaming around. The birds wasted no time climbing on top of the table and began feasting. Juan chased them away, but gave up when they kept coming back. The family, still in the water, laughed as they watched the chickens make short work of the leftovers. They knew they had finished with the food, so if the chickens wanted it, so be it.

A Moment in Time - Watching a couple in love

It began to rain, so we took the opportunity to have lunch at the pool restaurant. The family who were swimming also took cover in the restaurant. From where I sat, facing the mother and father, I noticed how much in love they seemed to be. They sat side by side, smiling and whispering to each other, while enjoying café and rum. It was all very heartwarming to watch.

When the doctor came to our room to give me another treatment, he invited us to his home for dessert and iced café after our dinner. The doctor was out seeing a patient when we arrived and a couple were waiting on his front patio for him, making me realize just how dedicated doctors in Cuba are. When he was finished with his patients, we were served flan de huevos and iced coffee, and had a lovely last visit.

For our last day in Las Terrazas we were invited to Barbara's for breakfast. She serves breakfast to guests as part of the hotel package, and because Juan had spent his last night there, she invited us all. We were welcomed by her husband, Cirilo, who told us anything we wanted was ours, and to feel at home. Our breakfast was wonderful, and it was obvious that Barbara had gone all out with the preparation

Carene and I were spending our last night in Cuba at Adelaida's casa, and had plans to take her out for dinner. After a warm welcome, we were told we would be sleeping in the room Adelaida shares with her sister. I didn't ask questions but later found why. On our last visit, Carene and I had been awakened in the middle of the night with noise coming from outside and I had mentioned it to Adelaida, not complaining, but merely making conversation. I certainly didn't expect her to give up her room for us.

Juan picked us up and we went to the French restaurant that Adelaida had recommended a couple of years previously. We were seated on the veranda of the beautiful old mansion and enjoyed a wonderful meal. Across the road from the restaurant is a small park dedicated to John Lennon, with a bronze statue of him sitting on a bench. We had a lot of fun taking posed pictures, making them look as though we were sitting and having a conversation with him.

It was a beautiful evening so Juan, Carene and I decided to walk over to the Hotel Nacional for drinks and say our good-byes. We sat out on the rock and it was a perfect end, to a perfect last night, of a perfect vacation. Juan told us he loved us both.

Carene relayed a story Juan told her while I was walking Adelaida to her apartment. He said, at home that afternoon, Mari said he seemed sad and asked if he was OK. He told Carene that he was sad because we were leaving, and he was going to miss us. It was very touching to hear. Not only do I appreciate Juan and all he does for us, but the feeling is mutual.

Observations and Reflections - 2013

There are many changes taking place in Cuba, one being free enterprise is now allowed. There are now some new, privately run restaurants, offering good meals at reasonable prices.

Cuban people are used to dealing with obstacles. When they run up against one, they might be down for a while, but before long they stand up, dust themselves off, and go on.

When a tourist messes up, like I did by forgetting our concert tickets, the people in charge go out of their way to make things right. Not only were the forgotten tickets honoured, but a woman from the entrance ushered us to our seats and wished us well.

October 2013

People You'll Meet

Henry Aloma - Artist

Mario Pelegrin - Artist and Coordinator of El Patio de Pelegrin

Chapter Twenty-One

This trip, suggested to me by Barbara, I travelled to Cuba alone, to spend the entire time in Las Terrazas, staying at Barbara's, while Juan stayed in the house next door that also offered community housing.

Juan picked me up in Varadero, and he had his son with him, to allow him to practise his driving skills. We stopped in Mantanza for lunch and, after dropping Juan's son off in Havana, continued on to Las Terrazas.

After freshening up, we went to El Romero for something to eat. It had been a long day of travelling so it was nice to finally relax.

Before heading to bed, I decided to take advantage of my outdoor shower. After taking some time to get organized, I was ready. It was then that I realized the outdoor shower had only cold water. My shower was a short one, but it certainly did refresh me. I climbed into my comfortable bed, and in the pitch black with not a sound to be heard, drifted off into a peaceful sleep.

The next day, on a walk around the village, we happened upon a gallery in a house close to Barbara's. As we looked around the small studio, the artist, Henry Aloma, appeared. He was a young man of about thirty and spoke English, so we had a nice conversation. Thinking his pictures would make good Christmas presents, I told him I would be back another day to purchase some. Next, we stopped at a house where Juan had stayed the previous April. It is run by a woman, but her grandfather, a man of ninety-three, acts as a greeter of sorts. He must have been relaxing before we arrived, because as we spoke he was discreetly buttoning his shirt, not wanting to greet guests in his undershirt. After giving me a tour of the room they rent, he presented me with a basket he had made of palm bark.

Yamelis came to Barbara's for a visit and told us that the doctor was in Brazil on a contract for three years. He would make trips home every eleventh month, staying for one month. Since the house he and Yamelis had resided in was now occupied by the new doctor for Las Terrazas, Yamelis was living with her parents. I invited her and her family to join me for dinner the next evening at El Romero, telling her that Barbara, Cirilo and Rye would also be joining us.

Barbara had invited Juan and me to have dinner with her and her family that night. I found it to be quite a compliment that they were so welcoming. Dinner was fantastic, and it was obvious Barbara had been cooking all day. During dinner, the subject of our plans for the next evening came up, and I learned they were declining my invitation. With embarrassment, they said they weren't fussed on vegetarian, and when they had eaten there, they always left hungry. I told them we could go somewhere else, but they said they didn't want me to change my plans. Later, Juan told me it was mainly Cirilo who didn't want to go, and Barbara and Rye didn't want to go without him. He explained that El Romero has evenings for the locals, allowing them to pay in Cuban pesos, but apparently on those evenings the menu is limited. Barbara and Rye said that they would try and change Cirilo's mind.

A Moment in Time - Walking from Barbara's to Hotel Moka

With the night sky inky black, and lights few and far between, we walked with flashlights in hand, the few steps from Barbara's kitchen door to a staircase that leads down to a valley bottom between terraces. Crossing over a small stream on a concrete foot bridge, we manoeuvered around some mud on a low spot, then climbed more stairs to the top of a terrace. On that level, a road circles part of the village where row housing, as well as Café Maria's, Fonda de Mercedes, and El Romero are located. Across the road, loom the longest set of stairs to tackle before reaching the hotel. Halfway up, some benches provide a resting spot, and a floral shrub fills the air with the most beautiful perfume imaginable. By now, there are usually strange wheezing noises escaping from my body, and I can count on hearing Juan tell me, "Easy Bonnie, easy Bonnie." When the concrete stairs turn into stone steps, I know we've almost reached our destination. After making a turn, we are at the base of the hotel. We climb a short set of wooden stairs, turn, and climb another set that take us to the lobby level. One short flight up is the bar, and by now, I need a drink!

Being a Saturday, a lot of the folks from Las Terrazas were at home, so Juan suggested as a way to practise my Spanish, we would walk around the community, approach people, introduce myself, and try to converse with them.

First, we went up to the town square where a small market was set up with local people selling their wares. Las Terrazas is trying to improve the community, making it an even more desirable place to visit. In the three years since I first visited, I've witnessed quite a few changes, the biggest being an addition to Hotel Moka. Another is a second, larger location, just off the town square for Café Maria. With the original spot having only five tables, it was just too small to accommodate the many bus tours that stop in the village for café.

In a section of the village where I hadn't been, we came upon a man trying to persuade some ducks to go down to the water. He told us he was a musician, and later would be performing with his band at a near-by coffee plantation. Since we were planning on going there for lunch, we said we would see him there. He then asked if we would like to see his small botanical garden. We walked down a couple of steps, and I couldn't believe my eyes. The man had taken old pieces of junk and welded things together, turning everything into a small gym. There were plants galore, all lush and beautiful, as well as birds in cages, all accented with different metal sculptures he'd made. A dog resided happily in a house made out of an old oil drum, placed in a shady spot. Our host explained that he had built the whole thing in his spare time because he loves plants.

We walked on and I approached different people speaking to them in Spanish. At first I received some blank stares, but when they figured out what I was trying to do, they would smile, and in the Cuban way, invite us to sit down, and offer café.

There are a few abandoned coffee plantations in the area of Las Terrazas, one of them being the Buena Vista. It has been restored and now contains a restaurant. At the plantation, all the buildings, a wall surrounding them, as well as a large patio out behind the main house are made of stone. It's truly mind boggling to imagine how many man-hours would have gone into the construction of it all. Not far from the main house is an area sectioned off into large squares where the beans used to be laid out to dry in the sun. Behind is a grinder - a large wooden disk, attached to an equally large pole, and set in a circular trough. The slaves walked in a circle, pushing the pole, making the attached disk rotate in the trough, grinding the beans. The remains of slave quarters, also made of stone, are where whole families lived in small rooms, making it evident just how brutal the living conditions were.

A Moment in Time - Saturday afternoon in Las Terrazas

After a siesta, we decided to go to Café Maria's new location in the town square for our afternoon café. Upon entering the square, everything we saw seemed to be a picture. The old gentleman who we had visited earlier sat on a bench at the edge of the square, having a quiet moment while gazing out at the beauty before him. At a table nearby, some men were playing a game of dominos, while others sat visiting over café in Café Maria.

The people of Las Terrazas built an outdoor water feature – like a shower really – with flowing water on three sides. Every Saturday, the water is turned on for a few hours to allow the children of the community to play. If you give children water to play in, they will be happy for hours and, judging by the gales of laughter I was hearing, the children of Las Terrazas certainly loved their water feature. Their mothers stood nearby, chatting, quite content to let the children play while they visited.

Barbara and Rye had managed to persuade Cirilo to attend the dinner I was hosting at El Romero. There would be nine of us in total, and I was looking forward to it. I had seen Barbara having her hair done earlier, and Rye doing her nails, so I felt they were also looking forward to the evening.

When my guests arrived at the restaurant, the first thing they did was walk to the kitchen to greet the owner and the staff. Cirilo asked the owner, "Am I going to feel full after this meal?" After everyone was seated and drinks were ordered, I said a few words in Spanish, telling them how much I love Las Terrazas and thanked them for welcoming me into their community. I kidded Cirilo, telling him that I had arranged to have a pig delivered to the restaurant just for him. Dinner was a lot of fun with everyone laughing and joking. Cirilo teased the two youngest girls by stating, "I hope you're full, because you sure ate a lot!" They had begun the meal with a bun with cheese and vegetables, and for a second course had pasta. A full entrée followed and they finished their meal with ice cream. When dinner was over we took some group photos, and after many hugs and kisses said good-night.

The day we were going to the Río San Juan, was a little overcast so we didn't take our bathing suits, but thought we would have lunch and just spend some time in the park. After lunch, as we sat on a log with our feet in the water, surrounded by the incredible beauty of the river, a feeling of peacefulness washed over me, rejuvenating my body, as well as my spirit.

We had been invited to dine again with Barbara and her family so that I could experience a Sunday dinner, Cuban style. When I came out of my room, Juan and Cirilo were watching a TV program that reminded me of the Ed Sullivan show, which aired for years on Sunday nights at home. Cirilo said the program they were watching was a Sunday evening staple in Cuba. My thought was, we might come from different countries, but some things are very much alike.

Earlier in the day, Cirilo had come home with a breadfruit and showed it to me, explaining, they are good to feed to pigs because it enhances their breeding, but are also suitable for humans to eat. He said Barbara would prepare it for our dinner.

We dined on what has become my favourite Cuban dish, pork, done in sour oranges with spices and onions. It was accompanied with rice and red beans, malanga chips, fried breadfruit, yucca and salad. Malanga is a root vegetable, similar to a yam that is widely eaten in Cuba. Dessert was flan de huevos.

During dinner Barbara had to leave the room when she began to cough and I realized that she had a terrible cold. I'm sure the last thing she had felt like doing all day was to be in the kitchen cooking. She said her friend told her to put Vicks Vapor Rub on her feet and then wear socks to bed. The cure must have worked because she was much better the next day.

When we thanked the family for sharing their Sunday meal with us, Cirilo said they wanted to prepare dinner for us on Wednesday, which would be my last night in Las Terrazas. I was experiencing that familiar mushy feeling in my stomach again, while wondering if these people could be any sweeter.

Near Las Terrazas is a community project called El Patio de Pelegrin, owned and operated by a wonderful and giving artist, Mario Pelegrin. I first heard of the project the previous year when Jesús told me that he and Juan, along with an artist from California, had visited. Because Las Terrazas is only about an hour from the project, I thought this visit would be a good time for me to check it out. After visiting the patio, we would continue on to Pinar del Río, the capital city of the province we were in.

We pulled up to a house with a quirky and colourful mural painted on the front façade, and were met at the gate by a friendly woman who remembered Juan from his previous visit. She told him that a bus tour was expected shortly, so we could tour the project with them, adding that Mario was waiting for the tour to arrive, and we could find him outside the gallery. We followed winding paths all decorated with mosaic work, and found Mario. He was very happy to see Juan and said that he would like us to be his guests for lunch.

Patio Pelegrin offers free workshops for children from the community where they learn painting, ceramics, clay work, dance and theatre, to name but a few. Mario brings in teachers, some of whom are older, for the dance and theatre, and they teach the children to dance son, a traditional type of music and dance in Cuba.

The tour group arrived and Mario gave a short talk. These visitors were from Austria and Switzerland, so as their tour guide translated into German, Juan whispered to me in English.

We entered a small gallery with paintings on display by different artists. I purchased one of a Cuban peasant, smoking a big cigar, whose eyes seemed to follow me. In a lending library, some small pieces that had been made by the children were for sale. Exiting the library, we walked amid lush greenery, to see old artifacts on display, birds and small animals in cages, and even an alligator. A cabana had been built, with plans to build three more, so that visiting artists could stay at Pelegrin if they wished. Juan and I climbed the ladder to the cabana, and it all looked quite comfortable. Behind the patio, a large vegetable garden containing every type of vegetable imaginable had obviously been tended with care. The land, where the garden was, had been given to the project by the state. It had been full of trash, but with the help of volunteers, was cleaned up and put to good use.

By the time we returned to the patio, tables had been set up and a beautiful lunch awaited us. There was pork loin in sour oranges, morro, malanga and salad. An array of desserts included fried ripe bananas, sweet coconut balls, and a type of bread pudding made with honey called *torreja*, which I loved. Because Juan and I were at a small table by ourselves, the woman who greeted us initially fussed over us. When she realized how much I liked the torreja, she wrapped some up for me to take home and told me how to make it. While we ate, a gentleman sang along with pre-taped music, which was a nice added touch. After the meal, we were invited to a small café on the patio for café if we wished. It was charming, with a few tables and brightly painted walls, covered with messages written by previous visitors.

A Moment in Time - Watching Mario's pet Gavilan

After the tour group left, we were invited up to Mario's apartment to visit. As I climbed the stairs I could see a large, mean-looking bird sitting on the landing, eating a piece of raw chicken. He would knead the meat with his talons and then tear a small piece off and eat it. Nobody seemed to be paying much attention to him, so I just walked past him to Mario's upper balcony. One end of the balcony was set up for a studio, while the other end held chairs and many birds in cages. As we sat chatting, the bird came walking down the hall of the apartment toward us, still holding his piece of chicken. Juan explained that Mario had hand-raised the bird, called a Gavilan, since it was a chick. It stood at Mario's feet while finishing the chicken, and when he was done, spread his talons, cleaned them with his beak, then flew up into a tree beside the balcony and sat there.

As we were leaving we walked past the main house where some older people were sitting on a patio in rocking chairs. Mario introduced us to his mother, who smiled broadly at me, then took my hand telling me how much she loved her son.

In Pinar del Río we walked around taking in the sights and I found the architecture to be quite interesting. There is a large cigar factory there, so I took the opportunity to purchase some cigars and rum.

In the morning, Barbara knocked on my door to tell me that the hotel was putting on a dinner at the pool that evening, and Juan and I were invited to attend. They were going to cook creole food, and there would be some live music.

We didn't have much planned for the day, so decided to go for a walk. We came upon a group of older people sitting under a palapa in rocking chairs, and I realized this was the senior's daycare centre where we had been in 2011, but at that time hadn't known what it was. I introduced myself in Spanish, and we were invited to sit down. A younger woman, holding a copy of Granma, was just about to read the paper to the seniors to keep them current with the news. She told us she was a historian for Las Terrazas and was writing a book about the area. I said I thought a book was a good idea since Las Terrazas is such a unique place, with a very interesting history. We had a nice visit with the seniors, with them relaying stories of how long they had lived in the area, and how difficult life had once been there.

Back at Barbara's, during another Spanish lesson, I wondered if I'd ever master the language. Incorporating small words into everyday speaking seemed to be challenging me the most. Juan gave me a tip, telling me, during the day, to say everything I'm doing in Spanish. For example, I would say, "I got out of bed and went to the bathroom, where I washed my face and brushed my teeth." I was to say everything, using the words I was having difficulty with. He said when he was studying English that is what his professor had suggested to the class.

For lunch, we were going to walk over to where the buses travelling to Pinar del Río and Viñales make a rest stop. It is quite a nice spot with a small lake, Lago El Palmar, as well as a canteen, Rancho Curejey. The town offices are also located here, and I wanted to deliver a letter I had written.

On our way, we passed the school, and the children were outside on their lunch break. Juan said it would be okay to enter the school yard and talk with them. Walking around the yard, I noticed some differences between a school yard in Cuba and ones in Canada. One thing that stood out was a horse, lying under a tree, beside the school. I guess in Cuba you can ride your horse to school instead of a bicycle. There were two young girls shooting marbles, and a short distance away a couple of girls played cards on a tree stump. At a table, a teacher was teaching some children how to play dominoes.

At Rancho Curejey, the tables and chairs are outdoors, overlooking Lago El Palmar, making it a nice spot to sit and have either a drink or something to eat. The canteen was empty when we entered, and the three staff members were sitting and chatting. They basically ignored us which annoyed Juan, and things went downhill from there. We waited a while, and when no one came to the table, Juan motioned for the waiter. He told us all they had to offer were Cuban sandwiches, so we ordered two. Cuban sandwiches are ham, cold roast pork, cheese and sliced dill pickles on Cuban bread and grilled. The waiter never asked if we wanted anything to drink, so Juan went to the counter and ordered. The waiter put the drinks on the counter then disappeared into the kitchen, so a gentleman selling souvenirs brought the drinks to us. I have no idea why the server gave us such poor service, perhaps he just took a dislike to us, but he certainly didn't receive much of a tip from me.

After we finished our lunch, we went to the town offices to deliver my letter. I explained who I was, and where I was from, and went on to say that I loved Las Terrazas. I praised them for the positive changes they had made, to let them know they hadn't gone unnoticed. I also suggested that the history of Las Terrazas be put into a book to sell to tourists. I had written the letter before learning that a book was in the works, but I thought my comment couldn't hurt.

A Moment in Time - A loyal friend

Walking back toward the village, we came upon two women and a dog, also walking in our direction. When a passing car stopped for the women, they jumped in and the car drove off. I thought the dog would return to where he had come from, but instead he began running after the car. Juan said that the dog would run after the car until he caught up with his master. The distance is only about one kilometre so, thank goodness, he didn't have too far to run.

Juan and I walked up to the hotel pool for the dinner we had been invited to. The dinner was good but was regular Cuban fare, not Creole like they had claimed. I think they call their food Creole whenever they add a little spice to it.

The same band was playing that we had seen at the coffee plantation a few days before. As is the custom, when a band is on a break, one of the members goes around selling their CD. I wanted to purchase one and couldn't figure out why we weren't being approached. Juan motioned the musician over and they had a conversation in Spanish. The band member said he assumed Juan was a *jinetero*, or gigolo, and I was a paying client, so he didn't want to infringe on Juan's action. It upset me a little, but I decided to not concern myself. Let people think what they want. Perhaps that explained the poor service we had received at Rancho Curejey.

After dinner, we went to the bar in the hotel. It was pretty quiet when we arrived, but when a large group of tourists came in, things quickly livened up. They began asking the band to play some Elvis because the men wanted to sing. The band obliged and the men lined up and began putting on quite a show. I was finding it quite funny that the group was in Cuba, which is known for its music, were requesting Elvis.

In most groups that socialize together, there is usually an organizer. The organizer in this group was a woman who just didn't stop. Perhaps to keep her occupied, the band gave her some claves, wooden cylinders that are played by striking them together. The problem was she had absolutely no sense of rhythm. One of the band members kept trying to help her find the beat, and she was concentrating, but to no avail. By then, both Juan and I were cracking up. All of a sudden, Juan blurted out to me, "That's it, I'm going to take her out and put her in front of a firing squad!"

We talked to some of the group and learned they were from Essex, England. They had been all over Cuba, and after leaving Las Terrazas, would finish their tour with five days in Varadero. Walking back to our casas we commented on what a fun night it had been.

On my last full day in Las Terrazas since I can't get enough of the chicken at El Campesino, I told Juan I wanted to go there for lunch.

The restaurant was full with bus tours when we arrived, so we were seated on the front porch of the farm house with a couple from Nashville, Tennessee, and their taxi driver. The man, a doctor specializing in lung problems, travels all over the world speaking, which he had been doing in Havana. With a day off, they decided to hire a taxi and explore some of the area.

A Moment in Time - Running into an old amigo

I saw a tour bus in the parking lot from Amistad, the tour company that The View worked with when I volunteered. When the driver left the bus, I recognized him to be our driver, Angel. Since Angel speaks no English, I had Juan accompany me to say hello. It had been eight years since we had seen each other, but he remembered me. When he told me he looked a little older, I assured him I did as well. He asked about the leaders from The View, and then thanked me for returning to Cuba, which I thought was very sweet. Here I was in a country far from home, running into an old amigo. The expression, "It's a small world" came to mind.

A Moment in Time - Experiencing paradise on earth

While we were eating lunch it began to pour rain. The sound of the rain as it bounced off the lush greenery was music to my ears. As I sat in this beautiful place, enjoying one of my favourite Cuban dishes, I was in heaven.

Although we were the only customers left, I wasn't ready to leave, so we ordered another mojito. When Juan left me to use the washroom, I sat alone in the quiet, lost in thought. My heart was full. With the leaves and flowers sagging from the weight of raindrops clinging to them, and the air smelling fresh and sweet, I could feel the angels around me.

We had been invited for a special dinner at Barbara's for my last night, so after a siesta, I showered and dressed up. As an added treat with dinner, we were served papa renellas, or stuffed potatoes. I had asked Barbara one day if she made them, telling her how much I loved them. Even though potatoes weren't in season, somehow Cirilo had managed to find some. When I realized that both Juan and I had two papa renellas on our plates, while the family had only one each, I made an excuse that I had eaten a big lunch and asked Cirilo if he would like my second one. During dinner Barbara told me, "This time tomorrow night I'll be missing you." Through tears, I managed to tell her that I would miss her too. I was going to miss everything about Las Terrazas.

Juan and I were walking to the hotel for our last night when an odd thing happened. After crossing the concrete foot bridge in the valley, a horse that I hadn't seen, snorted loudly, making me jump out of my skin. I'm sure my scream scared the horse as much as it had scared me. That will give you an idea of just how dark it gets in Las Terrazas.

At the bar, we ordered two Mira de Las Terrazas and toasted our successful venture together. The band was playing and before long the group from England arrived, just as wound up as they had been the night before. The party was in full swing, with everyone having a good time, when the bartender announced she had run out of ice. We took it as a sign to call it a night as we had an early morning ahead of us. When I told the bartender it was my last night in Las Terrazas and thanked her for her service, she gave me a kiss and a hug, telling me to return again.

Walking home, a light rain was falling, which Juan didn't like one bit. Thinking it felt very refreshing, I told him he wouldn't melt. As we climbed the last set of stairs to Barbara's I heard a man speaking and realized it was Cirilo. There he was, standing at the top of the stairs, holding an umbrella for me.

We had a three-hour drive to Varadero airport, so breakfast was early. As we were saying our final good-byes, I became teary-eyed. Not only had this family showered me with kindness, they had treated us to three dinners in their home. I knew they wouldn't take money if I offered it, so along with a note of thanks I left some money in my room.

More Observations and Reflections - 2013

It seems there are many places where Sunday meals are special, which was the case with the one at Barbara's.

I consider myself fortunate to be able to experience Cuba the way I do. After spending eight days in an out-of-the-way place, with people who love life, show great respect for each other, and look after their elders, I came away with a refreshed outlook on mankind.

Section Eight

May 2014

Music at El Tanque, Muraleando – 2014

Juan, Carene, Sancti Spíritus – 2014

Chapter Twenty-Two

On this trip I would be accompanied by my niece Miriam, visiting Cuba for the first time. Juan picked us up in Varadero, and after stopping in Mantanza for lunch, we drove directly to Las Terrazas. We would stay there for three nights, Miriam and I at Hotel Moka, and Juan with Barbara in community housing.

We awoke to a beautiful day, so after breakfast the three of us went for a walk to show Miriam what Las Terrazas was all about. We ran into the guide from a bird watching tour Juan and I had taken in 2011 and, after chatting a bit, he invited us to his home to meet his wife. Even though she was busy doing laundry we were offered café. Miriam was experiencing Cuban hospitality up close and personal.

We came upon the old gentleman Juan had once stayed with. Wearing his trademark white cowboy hat, he was busy gathering bark from palm trees to use for the baskets he makes.

At the town square, we visited the museum, where the history of the community was explained by a guide. As we pointed out the library and the cinema, a woman working in the cinema invited us in, telling us it isn't used much anymore because most people have DVD players in their homes. She laughed when I said that young people probably still like the cinema, as it allows them privacy to sit in the dark and smooch. Juan, being a photographer, found the old projectors particularly interesting.

Because Las Terrazas is growing, they now employ security guards to patrol the hotel grounds, as well as the town square. When Juan spoke with the security guard at the town square, he learned that Las Terrazas now had a money exchange, and Yamelis, the doctor's wife worked there. The guard happened to be a cousin of the doctor, so when Juan explained who we were, he offered to tell Yamelis we were there.

She was very surprised to see us, and filled us in on the doctor's news, saying they had enjoyed having him home for a month the past summer.

It was time to visit Café Maria to allow Miriam to experience her first café from there. While we sat drinking our café, a band member that we had come to know in November came to say hello, telling us that his band would be playing in the bar later. We had only been in Las Terrazas a short time, but judging by the friendly greetings we were receiving from everyone, I felt like I had come home.

It was still early, so we decided to go to the Río San Juan. We had lunch in the outdoor restaurant, and Miriam commented how good the chicken tasted. We were sitting with our feet in the water when a man came by offering horseback rides for 10 CUC an hour. Miriam had never been on a horse, so thought she'd give it a go. After receiving a quick lesson, she was on her way with a young guide, while Juan and I sat under a tree with a beer. An hour passed, and just as we began to wonder what was keeping the riders, they appeared. Because they had been gone longer than an hour, the owner of the horse tried to charge more than the original price quoted, but Miriam held firm. Months later, Miriam and I were re-living our Cuba trip, when I learned why the riders had been gone so long. The guide had been a little taken with Miriam. On the pretense of taking pictures of her with her camera, he kept stopping, telling her how beautiful she was, while stroking her face. Considering Miriam is probably ten years older than the guide, I found it all quite funny.

Dinner was at Fonda de Mercedes which serves traditional Cuban fare, and according to the locals is the best place to eat. It didn't disappoint and, because the restaurant is open-aired, it's a very pleasant place to dine. After dinner we went to the hotel bar, thinking we would hear some music, but the band had finished early, and were now in the lobby talking. Because bands in Cuba rely solely on tips, when things are quiet, they don't stick around. Three of them did stay and play for us, and one of them even taught Miriam how to dance salsa. Even though it was a quiet night, we had fun.

Miriam works in the food industry, with coffee being one of her specialties, so we thought that she would find the Buena Vista coffee plantation interesting.

From there, we drove to Puerto de Golpe, the small town where Patio Pelegrin is located. Juan had arranged for us to tour the patio and have lunch with Mario. After showing Miriam around the patio, we walked out behind to the large vegetable garden which was thriving. Behind it, at the back of the property, men were working on a building which would become a ceramic workshop as well as a studio for painting. It had mainly been funded by a large donation from Spain. Next to it, finishing touches were being put on a cabin where visiting artists could stay. The cabin, complete with washroom facilities, was utterly charming.

A table had been set for lunch on Mario's upper balcony. We enjoyed lobster tails, done in a tomato sauce, morro, sweet potato, and a salad of tomatoes and green beans in a vinaigrette dressing. Dessert was toronja, made with papayas, served with grated cheese on top and café finished off the delicious meal. While we visited, Mario told us he would be visiting Spain and then Canada in a few months. He had been to Canada once before and loved it. He kidded with Juan, telling him that he should accompany him to act as a translator. It all sounded like a fine idea to me but Juan wasn't biting.

When Mario was asked what I owed him for lunch, he replied he could never take my money, after all, I was considered family, and his casa is my casa. When I hear words like that, my heart melts. I gave him a donation for the project, and thanked him for a wonderful day. As we were leaving Mario gave both Miriam and me a gift of a painting, telling me to write to him and to bring more people to his patio.

A Moment in Time - A quiet moment

That night, I found myself ready for dinner with time to spare, so took the opportunity to go outside and enjoy the evening. As I sat on a bench not far from our rooms, the only sound was from a few birds, not ready to call it a day. I drank it all in – the quiet, the smells, and the beauty, and thought how fortunate I was to have discovered this beautiful and serene place.

For our last night in Las Terrazas we had dinner at El Romeo. I indulged in a daiquiri made with fresh papaya juice, which was so good, I ordered a second. We took a walk, gazing at the bright stars in the night sky, and then went to the hotel for drinks. When I was paying the bill, I was trying to speak Español. When the bartender told me the amount I owed, I drew a total blank, probably due to the daiquiris. I'm sure he thought he was dealing with a complete idiot. When I told Juan I had just made a fool of myself, and asked him how to say stupid in Spanish, he replied *estúpido*, which cracked the bartender up.

Today, we would be leaving Las Terrazas, and I certainly wasn't in a hurry to go. After breakfast, we went to Café Maria for our last café then took a walk, stopping on a bridge to look at monkeys that dwell on their own little island. Because it was Mother's Day week-end, Las Terrazas was a hive of activity. Buses were coming into the village, and many people were walking around. Juan explained that in low season, the state offers one-day bus tours for Cubans for 20 CUC. They include the bus, time at the river, and a meal at a restaurant of their choice in Las Terrazas. It was all making me wish that I could stay for another day.

We ended up at the boat house, and Juan said he would go and retrieve the car while Miriam and I had a cold drink. The boat house was busy with visiting Cubans, and I never tire of observing them enjoying life. Two couples had rented a rowboat and were attempting to go for a turn on the lake. The problem was the fellow manning the oars had no idea what he was doing. As the boat went in circles, the poor woman sitting in the bow was getting soaked whenever the oars slapped the water, which was pretty much occurring constantly. A man on the dock yelled orders, but between the screams from the woman, and all the laughter from the onlookers, including us, I'm not sure he could hear anything.

We decided that since Miriam hadn't experienced El Campesino, and we really weren't in a hurry to leave, we would have lunch there before heading to Havana. It was a perfect ending to a glorious few days in my favourite place on earth.

On the drive, I asked Miriam if she was ready for Havana, saying it was not at all like Las Terrazas, but crowded and noisy. When she just smiled, I knew she would be fine.

Chapter Twenty-Three

We would be staying in Havana's oldest hotel, the Hotel Inglaterra. I had been to their roof top bar a few times, but had never stayed there. The hotel has only three floors and some reviews stated that the lower two floors can be noisy so, I asked Juan if he would go to the hotel for me and try and pull a few strings. I wanted two rooms on the third floor at the front of the hotel. When he made my request, he told them that I visit Cuba frequently, so if I was pleased with the rooms, I would definitely be a repeat customer. The hotel accommodated us nicely.

Today was Mother's Day and, with mothers being held in such high regard in Cuba, I knew celebrating it here would be a memorable experience.

When I had been corresponding with Juan about the trip, I told him that I didn't want to interfere in anyone's celebration and we would be fine spending the day on our own. He wrote back telling me not to worry, and to "come and share the mother's cake", so I left it in his hands.

When Juan and Jesús picked us up for the day, Juan presented me with a Mother's Day card from him and Mari. In Cuba, they sell postage-paid postcards for Mother's Day that people can purchase to send to their mother. My card from Juan and Mari is among my most cherished possessions.

While touring the city, we went to a park on the river which is very lush and beautiful. When a car parked near us and Jesús noticed a man removing a burlap sack from the trunk, he remarked that we might witness a Santería ceremony. I don't know much about Santería, but knew that some ceremonies involve sacrificing animals. I was curious, but at the same time, I didn't want to witness a bird having its throat slit. Four people walked to the river and the ceremony began. I wanted to be respectful, so I stood back behind a tree while I observed. I didn't actually see birds being killed, but did see them float by, minus their heads. Juan explained that the Orisha asks for blood, either from a chicken or a goat. The animals are sacrificed to the river, where the current carries them away.

We drove to Old Havana, and while on a walking tour we came upon what I thought to be a bronze statue. As we stood looking at the statue, Jesús commented, "He won't move until you put a coin into his box." When he dropped in a coin and the statue began moving in a robotic way, I just thought it was automated. It wasn't until the statue extended his hand to Jesús that I finally realized what was up. I went over and the statue took my hand and kissed it, saying in halting English, "Happy Day of the Mother." I found the whole experience to be a little unnerving.

I didn't think we would be visiting Muraleando on Mother's Day, but I learned that some festivities were planned and we were invited to attend. Two bus tours were going to be visiting, with the second one staying for dinner and a party after.

The first tour was being shown around when we arrived and we were welcomed by some of my friends. I gave Miriam a tour of El Tanque, noticing that many changes had been made since my last visit, reminding me just how hard the artists and friends of Muraleando work for the cause.

As we looked at the murals on the Boulevard of Friendship, I was pleased to see MC Mario was conducting the tour. He had married a German woman and moved there, so I hadn't seen him for a couple of years. When he brought the tour into El Tanque, he greeted me, explaining to the tour that I was a Godmother of Muraleando.

The second tour of the day arrived and basically did the same as the first. Later, we were all asked to go to a room that had been set up for the dinner and sat down to a marvelous meal. After dinner Manolo gave a short speech and then asked the women who had spent their Mother's Day cooking to take a bow. When Mayra was asked by one of the guests what the secret was to the pork loin we had been served, she said that Muraleando was thinking of putting out a cook book with some of their recipes. I thought it was a very good idea since the food there is some of the best I've ever eaten. We were then invited to go up to the roof for café, and then the party would begin.

The day in Muraleando had been beyond wonderful, and I was pleased that Miriam's first visit had been so.

After another day of touring, we ended up on The Veranda of the Hotel Nacional for café. In all the times I had spent there, I really hadn't taken advantage of everything the hotel has to offer. Today, thanks to Jesús, that would change.

The Hall of Fame is where pictures of famous people who have stayed in the hotel over the years hang, arranged by decades, from the thirties to the present. We had a lot of fun naming the old stars and famous people. Next, we toured some trenches where Cuba had prepared to defend itself during the Cuban Missile Crisis in 1962.

I wanted to linger at the hotel, so told Jesús that Miriam and I were going to stay for a while. We sat out on the rock, enjoying the sunshine and the view, while sipping mojitos.

We had plans to have dinner with Juan and then do some bar hopping in Old Havana. When I met Miriam in the lobby and saw her above-the-knee boots and mini dress, I knew Juan and I would be fending off lots of men throughout the evening.

At the restaurant, when it came time to order, Miriam thought that she might like the pork chop. She said she wasn't too hungry so she asked the waiter how big the chop was. When the food arrived, we realized what the waiter neglected to tell her was that she would receive three chops. The look on her face was priceless, and she quietly said, "Now that's a lot of pork."

After dinner we walked into Old Havana and made our first stop at The Floridita, Ernest Hemingway's favourite watering hole. There is a life-size statue of him at the bar where he liked to sit. It was very busy so we took seats at the bar and ordered daiquiris, which The Floridita is known for. Legend has it that Hemingway invented the daiquirí at a bar called Sloppy Joes, in Key West, Florida. Others believe the drink was invented by an American mining engineer, Jennings Cox in Oriente Cuba as early as 1898.

For our last day, we toured a cigar factory, and went to Finca La Vigía, Hemingway's home in Cuba.

At lunch, when Jesús ordered a pizza, one of the ingredients he chose was olives, saying that he wondered what olives would taste like on a pizza. I assumed olives on pizzas were something new in Cuba. They put the olives on whole, so as well as rolling around, they look a little like eyeballs staring at you.

As we were walking back to the car, I saw a man on the sidewalk dressed completely in pink – pink shoes, pink pants and a pink shirt. I commented that he must really like pink.

Miriam and I went back to the hotel to get ready for a night of music at Patio Egrem, and decided to walk across the street to the Parque Central Hotel for our afternoon café. While drinking our café, I saw another man dressed all in pink. He wore pink shoes with pink laces, pink shorts and a pink Hawaiian shirt. Later, at Patio Egrem, there was another man dressed in pink. This was beginning to blow my mind, so I asked Juan what was the significance of the men in pink. He gave me a blank stare, telling me he thought it was merely a fashion statement. I felt there had to be more to it but have had no luck finding out what it is. In hindsight, I don't know why I didn't just ask the man at Patio Egrem.

Patio Egrem had undergone a major transformation since I had been there. It had gone from a bar with cement floors and plastic tables and chairs, to a very nice air conditioned club. We were going to hear one of the oldest bands in Cuba, Septeto Habanero, mainly made up of older gentlemen, who dress in suits and ties and wear straw fedoras.

As people arrived, it seemed many of them knew each other, so before sitting down, they'd greet each other. As I've said before, the way Cuban people greet each other is something I never tire of observing. Most Cubans don't order mixed drinks at a club, but rather, buy a bottle of rum for the table. They receive glasses and a dish of ice, along with some cola for those who want it. As the rum kicks in, the dancing gets more intense.

The band was fantastic. One of the oldest members, known for his bongo playing, wasn't playing, I assumed because of his age. Later in the evening, when he did play, I was in awe. He had to be in his mid-eighties, and was the epitome of cool.

Juan dropped us off in Barrio Chino then went to pick up Maria and Jenny, so we could all have dinner together. Just as we finished our meal, a musician who was strolling around the restaurant playing a violin made eye contact with me. He came to the table and stood between Maria and me and began playing classical music, basically playing right into Maria's ear. I could tell by the look on her face that she wasn't enjoying it much. One or two songs would have been okay, but he just kept on playing. It was another one of those times when I was clued out, not realizing he wanted money. It was like he was holding us hostage – give me money or I'll just keep playing. After he said something to Jesús in Spanish, Jesús asked me, "Bonnie, do you think you could contribute a couple of coins to support Cuban music?" I might be slow, but when I finally clued in, I couldn't get money out fast enough. When he moved on, we all breathed a sigh of relief.

Juan and Jesús picked us up at ten o'clock and we arrived at the Varadero airport with time to spare. After saying our good-byes and checking in, we sat and ordered chicken sandwiches and our last Cuban café, while we talked about what a wonderful holiday it had been.

Observations and Reflections - 2014

Being in Cuba is like taking a step back in time to an era that I remember fondly.

Cuban people always take great pride in their appearance. When they go out for an evening, they dress in their finery.

All over Cuba, different aspects of socialism are evident. In restaurants, you rarely see a worker trying to look busy when a boss is near. With everyone being equal, no one worries about such things. In places of historical importance and museums, the state employs people to act as guides. I'm sure there are days when no one visits.

Upon reflection, I realized that I have had three profoundly spiritual moments while in Cuba, all taking place in Las Terrazas. I know why I consider it to be my favourite place on earth.

October/November - 2014

Chapter Twenty-Four

Carene and I were having another Cuban adventure, taking a road trip with Juan, visiting some new places as well as some familiar ones. Our first destination would be Cienfuegos, where we would spend two nights at Bella Perla, a casa where Juan and I had stayed in 2011. When Juan was reserving Bella Perla, the owner, Waldo, advised him they had undergone a major renovation and now offered a "suite room". After viewing some pictures, I reserved the suite for Carene and me, and a regular room for Juan.

We arrived in Cienfuegos late afternoon and were welcomed by Waldo and his wife. They wanted to show us their new renovation, so we climbed the stairs to what was once the rooftop where we had taken our meals. It was now a dining room with three tables, a bar, and a pool table. An open kitchen had been added, enabling the cooking to be done there, rather than in the kitchen of the house. Just off the dining room was our suite. A large room contained a king-size bed, as well as an antique dining set, a stereo and a fridge. Double doors led to a small balcony that overlooked the street. Off the main room, a large bathroom contained a double Jacuzzi tub, shower, sink and toilet. Stairs led to a mezzanine with two double beds and a door from there led to an outdoor area with an abundance of plants and an old fashioned double swing. Up another level was a lookout and a view of the city.

Waldo and his wife were very proud of their establishment and I could see why. I asked how long the renovation had taken and they said one year. They now employ seven people who cook, serve, and clean, as well as a man who keeps an eye on guests cars parked on the street at night. It was nice to see this hard-working couple's business thriving, and know that they are making their employees' lives better. I guess there is something to be said for free enterprise.

We took a short walk then went back to the casa for dinner and ordered mojitos from the bar. Dinner included the biggest lobsters I'd ever seen, with each of us receiving a whole one. Music played, and as we relaxed after dinner with another mojito, Waldo came and had a dance with Carene.

Two dogs reside at Bella Perla, Frank and Jetty. Frank pretty well runs the show, and because Jetty was in the family way, he was very protective of her. They aren't around while people are eating, but as soon as meals are finished they are allowed to roam freely. While we were still at the table, Frank approached, put his front paws on Juan's lap then laid his head against his chest. The display of affection was too cute for words.

Back in our suite, I gave Juan the gifts I had brought for him and Mari. I had also brought a gift for Waldo and his wife, so I went downstairs to give it to them. It was a piece of Blue Mountain Pottery that I thought would be a nice piece of Canadiana for them. They told me the piece would hold a place of honour in their parlour.

Breakfast was not only delicious, but we couldn't believe the amount of food we received. There was guava juice, fresh fruit, two kinds of cheese, scrambled eggs with ham, bread, pound cake and our choice of tea or café. Carene, who is a cheese lover, discovered a type of Cuban cheese that she fell in love with.

While we were out exploring Cienfuegos, a man approached Juan, telling him that some musicians and artists would be performing on Patio UNEAC later. The patio, considered to be the headquarters of some Cuban intellectuals, was a pleasant, shaded area with tables and chairs as well as benches. We ordered drinks from the bar and took seats under a big tree. A stage at the end of the courtyard was where the people taking part in the concert would perform, and judging by the number of people waiting to go on, I felt we were in for a treat. We enjoyed traditional music, as well as some *Trova*, considered the underground music in Cuba in the seventies.

After the concert, we walked down toward the water to have some lunch, and then went across the street to the Malecón. It was a beautiful clear afternoon. The water was like glass, and with the sun glistening on it, and large ships anchored here and there, it was a feast for the eyes.

Juan suggested that he could go back to the casa, pick up the car, then come back and pick us up so we could go for a drive. We drove to the end of the Malecón to the area known as Punta Gorda. A yacht club and many rental units quite close to the water give the area a resort like feel.

A Moment in Time - Fishing in Cuba

A group of young boys were fishing, not with rods, but using only a line. Judging by the number of fish lying on the wharf, it seemed rods weren't necessary. Lying amongst all the fish was a dog. As the dog's owner told Juan how much his dog loved fish, he threw him one. It was grabbed mid-air and after a couple of crunches was gone. The dog hadn't touched any fish until one was given to him, reminding me that in Cuba, animals, as well as children are very well behaved.

Shortly after we returned to the casa, Waldo and his wife knocked on our door and presented me with a CD of Cuban music, and a statue of a horse done by a local artist. They also had a few rings made by the same artist and told both Carene and me to choose one. It was a very nice gesture by very nice people.

A Moment in Time - A tale of Frank the kitten

On the day we arrived, we were standing on our balcony watching the activity on the street, when Carene noticed a tiny kitten hanging out on the sidewalk below. A small hole in the side of a building provided refuge, and some garbage on the street provided food. Carene named the kitten Frank and was quite concerned about his well-being. The next morning, she saw two men on their way to work stop and look at the kitten. One of them was wearing a white coat which meant that he was some sort of *médico*. At lunch, we saved some of our fish and chicken for Frank, but when we returned to the casa there was no sign of him. We assumed and also hoped that one of the men had come back and retrieved him.

Upon checkout, I was pleasantly surprised when I received the bill and saw the amount owing. The suite and a regular room for two nights, with breakfasts, dinners, and drinks came to 350 CUC. I felt it was money well spent.

We were travelling to Sancti Spíritus, with a short stop in Trinidad. I wanted to travel mainly on back roads to make the drive more interesting. Not far from Cienfuegos, we had to come to an abrupt stop when we came upon a cattlebeast standing right in the middle of the road, looking like he had no intention of moving. Juan honked the horn and the beast turned his head, looked at us, and then slowly lumbered to the side of the road.

When Juan was trying to find certain roads, he found that some of the signs pointing the way had been tampered with. On the sign pointing the way to Trinidad, someone had turned the arrow so that it pointed in the wrong direction. Apparently, the locals get some sort of enjoyment out of messing with tourists, but luckily Juan had taken the route before so he was on to the tricksters.

The highways in Cuba have checkpoints all along them, but so far we had never been stopped. Our luck was about to run out. As we travelled along happily, we were motioned to pull into one. Juan handed his papers to the officer, but judging by the amount of time things were taking, there seemed to be a problem. I could hear the officer on a radio and it seemed there was a mix-up with the car. Just as I was beginning to become a little concerned, things were straightened out and we were given the go-ahead.

When we arrived in Trinidad, Juan wanted to take us to a casa particular where he had stayed previously. We came to a barrier across the road that stops unnecessary traffic from driving on the narrow cobblestone streets in the older section of the city. Juan spoke to the guard and told him where we wanted to go, stretching the truth a little, saying we were expected. The guard made a phone call and spoke to someone, then handed the phone to Juan. Somehow the casa owner figured out what was up and went along, so the barrier was raised and we were on our way.

Even though it was a busy time, we were welcomed warmly. I think Juan had perhaps told the lady of the house that we might be future customers. She told him to go ahead and show us around and that we were welcome to have a cold drink if we'd like. Maids were scurrying around, no doubt getting the rooms ready for new customers. Sheets were everywhere, some in piles waiting to be washed and others hanging to dry in the bright sunlight. A man stopped what he was doing and made daiquiris for Carene and me, while our trusty driver settled for water.

We walked to the main square, Plaza Mayor, and had a quick look around, and then drove to the lookout at the Valley de los Ingeniousa, and on to the Manaca Iznaga Estate.

When we arrived back at the car, a man pointed out to Juan that one of the tires looked soft so we drove to a house that sold air and topped up the tire. In Cuba, air is found at homes where they are licenced to do tire repairs.

---

*Sancti Spíritus, population 100,000, and the provincial capital, is a very pretty city situated near the Yayabo River. Like Trinidad, it was also founded by Diego Velasquez in 1514. The town grew as sugar and livestock became important and its geographical position made it an excellent agricultural market town. It had been embellished with elegant mansions throughout the seventeenth and eighteenth centuries. Today it is a small attractive colonial centre that doesn't receive many visitors as most people just pass through on their way to other locations.

We entered the town crossing over the Yayabo Bridge, the oldest bridge in all of Cuba, and declared a national monument. I was quite pleased to be visiting Sancti Spíritus when I saw how charming it was. A large town square with benches all around the outside was obviously a meeting place. Another smaller square, not far from the main one, is where we found our hotel.

Hostal del Rijo is a 1818s mansion that has been converted into a small hotel containing sixteen large and attractive rooms. Our two rooms, side by side, both had balconies overlooking the square.

A Moment in Time - The worst sleep ever

I was ready for a good night's sleep, but it wasn't to be. I don't like sleeping in air conditioning so I took the bed closest to the balcony and left the doors open. I felt quite comfortable doing so as we were on the second floor, and the fellow that the hotel pays to watch the vehicles all night had his van parked right below our rooms.

The only pillows on the beds were bolsters and a couple of toss cushions. They were lovely to look at, but proved to be horrible to sleep on. After tossing and turning for a while I got rid of the bolster and tried one of the toss cushions but found it to be as hard as rock. I went and got a blanket out of the cupboard, folded it and gave that a go. It wasn't great but it was better than the neck-breaking bolster. Meanwhile, Carene was out cold in the next bed, oblivious to my dilemma.

While I was tossing around I could hear voices coming from outside. I got up to investigate and discovered that the man guarding the cars had a friend keeping him company and they were having their own private party, working hard to kill a bottle of rum. They weren't being overly loud, just loud enough to keep me awake.

In the morning I awoke to some noise coming from outside. I went to the balcony and saw a lot of school children gathered on the far side of the square. Juan told us when he had been on the street earlier he had seen children, all holding flowers and walking toward the Yayabo River. He remembered it was the day of remembrance for Camillo Cienfuegos.

A Moment in Time - Remembering Camillo Cienfuegos

Camillo Cienfuegos was a leading figure in the Cuban Revolution. On October 28, 1959, his plane mysteriously disappeared. No trace of Camillo or the plane was ever found.

Every year on October 28, school children all over Cuba toss flowers into the ocean or a body of water in remembrance of him.

When we came down for breakfast, Juan was speaking with one of the men from the hotel. He told us that he had been asked if he would mind moving to their sister hotel, which they said was close by. The man said they were expecting a big group and were short one room. Juan told him that he was comfortable where he was, not really giving him an answer. As we discussed the matter, we agreed that since we would be in and out all day, moving would just be an unnecessary complication for us. Later, when we returned to the hotel, Juan was asked again if he would move. I went to the desk, telling them that we had booked our rooms well in advance and that Juan was our guide, and I wanted him where he was, so he wouldn't be moving.

While exploring Sancti Spíritus, I was impressed by the cleanliness and loved its colonial feel. The town square was bordered by a church, a library and other official buildings, all painted in different bold colours with white trim. The business area had a boulevard closed to traffic that was decorated with sculptures and many plants in huge clay pots.

We stopped at a small museum, dedicated to Serafin Sanchez, a local patriot who took part in both Wars of Independence and was killed while fighting in 1896. The museum is located in the original family home and full of many interesting artifacts.

Sancti Spíritus has many horse-drawn vehicles so, since it was so hot, I suggested that we hire one to continue exploring the town. After a nice ride, we were dropped near the river where we visited a theatre, dating back to 1876, and took a short tour. There were some books and postcards for sale and I found a book of poems that had been translated into English. Since the guide only dealt in Cuban pesos, Juan bought the book for me. The price was equivalent to 50¢ – certainly a lot less than we would pay for a book like it in Canada. Because we were very close to the Yayabo Bridge the guide explained some of the bridge's history, telling us that when the bridge was being built, milk from goats had been mixed in with the mortar to strengthen it. Since the bridge had been built in 1815 and showed no signs of decay, the goats' milk must have worked.

On the town square we visited a church, Parroquial Mayor del Espiritu Santo, dating from 1522. It is acknowledged as the second oldest church in Cuba because it still stands on its original foundation. Finished in 1680, having taken sixty years to build, it is now a national monument. The church was under renovation when we visited, which seems to be quite common with churches in Cuba. Because they rely strictly on donations to pay for the work, it is a very slow process.

Breakfast was served on the front veranda which was a nice way to say good-bye to Sancti Spíritus. We lingered over café then I went inside to check out. The man at the desk figured everything out on the computer and told me I owed 350 CUC. He made no attempt to give me a receipt which made me wonder, but I didn't question him. That proved to be a huge mistake.

Days later, when the topic came up, I realized that I had been cheated to the tune of 70 CUC. Because Juan had reserved the Hostal del Rijo, I didn't know the price he had been quoted. He felt terrible, but I assured him it wasn't his fault and that I should have known to ask for a receipt. We decided that Juan would call Hostal del Rijo and tell them what had occurred. He would tell them that he is a tour guide and will never take clients there again. I said I would write to Trip Advisor and The Lonely Planet and advise them of the situation. I knew I'd never get my money back, but it was a lesson learned: Be vigilant at all times.

Sancti Spíritus is a beautiful town, but because most people only pass through on their way to another destination, it lacks choices for dining and entertainment.

Chapter Twenty-Five

Our drive from Sancti Spíritus to Havana was a long one, but interesting in many ways. We hadn't travelled far when we passed two young men in the grass beside the highway, whaling away on each other. I asked Juan if he thought they were having a serious fight or just fooling around and he replied that no, they weren't fooling around. I then asked if we should turn back and try to stop the fight, but he said no, that if we interfered they might turn on us, adding that before long they would probably be the best of friends again.

As we drove along, we began to hear a flapping noise coming from one of the tires. Juan pulled over and found that the tire that had been giving us trouble had a tear and was beginning to separate. We drove slowly to the next gas station but were told they didn't do tire work. They directed us to a place about five km down the road but when we arrived there Juan was told that the men who did tire work were at lunch and would be back in about twenty minutes. We had a decision to make – should we wait and hope the repair men would be back on time, or change the tire ourselves. Juan decided to change the tire himself. It was a wise decision because in the time it took him to change the tire we never did see the repair men return.

The rest of the trip was uneventful, and we arrived at The Hotel Inglaterra late afternoon. I gave Juan a big hug, telling him, "Good driving bud." I invited him to join us for dinner and asked if he thought Jesús would also like to join us. The four of us had a lovely dinner, catching up with Jesús and making plans for the next few days.

After a good night's sleep on a decent pillow, I was ready for a full day with Juan and Jesús.

Our first stop was The Museum of Nature and Man, located in Miramar and founded by J. Nunez Jimenez, a Cuban revolutionary and academic. He travelled the world, doing a lot of writing about his travels, and saved absolutely everything. The museum was full of many very interesting artifacts, and held several volumes of his writings. From there we visited a community project, also in Miramar, started by the artist Alexis Leiva Machado, who also goes by the name KCHO. The project was quite elaborate and Jesús told us that it helps the community a great deal.

Jesús wanted to take us to an exclusive beach club for visiting diplomats and their families. He knew the name of a woman working there who he had helped with real estate when she was relocating to Havana. At the gate, he used his charm and the woman's name, and we were granted permission to enter.

We walked toward the beach and found an area that looked like any up-scale resort, except it was almost empty. There was a sandy beach, two swimming pools, and a food booth. Jesús learned that for a modest sum, visitors could use the facilities for the day.

We entered a large building where meetings with diplomats are held. A security guard greeted us and Jesús inquired after his friend. We were directed to a lounge, and greeted by a very attractive and impeccably dressed young woman. When Jesús introduced himself, she welcomed us in and, in keeping with the custom in Cuba, said that she would like to offer us café.

The lounge, where diplomats could relax with a drink, or smoke a cigar, was furnished with leather furniture and a well-stocked bar. Beside the lounge, a separate temperature-controlled room held many different kinds of Cuban cigars available for purchase.

Palenque, a restaurant where everything is cooked over an open flame and one of Juan's favourites, was nearby so we went there for lunch. Carene and I ordered a pitcher of frozen sangria that was so good, we ordered a second. Like a lot of outdoor restaurants in Cuba, a cat wandered around, so Carene and I fed it. We found him to be quite uppity, bringing us to the conclusion that he was the best fed cat in Cuba.

At night we went to Patio Egrem to take in some live music and dance salsa. The band performing consisted of twelve men and they rocked the house, playing mainly son, which is a type of traditional Cuban music, and my favourite. As usual, it was a great time.

Leaving the building, I could hear drumming and music coming from across the street and saw people crowded around a house. I went to investigate and saw a drummer and a man dancing in a native style. Jesús said they were doing a Santería ceremony for a birthday and that the drumming and dancing would continue for hours.

Carene and I were spending the day alone, but Juan would join us later for dinner. It was nice to wake up and have a leisurely breakfast without having to be somewhere at an appointed time.

Breakfasts are included at most hotels in Cuba so, consequently, the higher priced the hotel is, the better the breakfasts. The Hotel Inglaterra, being a budget hotel has pretty basic breakfasts, but they are certainly adequate. Sometimes the buffet items aren't refilled as quickly as they might be, but when I'm in Cuba I don't concern myself with such things. On this particular day, because we went for breakfast later, a lot of the dishes were empty. While I sat waiting for the scrambled eggs to be replenished, I watched as a waitress filled a plate from the cold buffet, and then took it and put it into a drawer in the wait station. I think she was making sure that she was going to get her breakfast before everything was gone.

Just outside the hotel, we ran into Lazaro's mother, Mariela. It had been two years since I had visited the family, and when I approached her she was so shocked to see us that I thought she was going to cry. We tried to catch up on our news but, because of my limited Spanish, and Mariela's limited English, it was difficult. She invited us to her home for café later so we made arrangements for a five o'clock visit. Carene texted Juan and asked him to accompany us to translate.

We decided that we would walk down the Paseo del Prado to the Malecón, and then walk beside the water to the Hotel Nacional. We both love the grounds behind the hotel, and even though we weren't staying there, it would be nice to sit on The Veranda, or out on the edge of the rock and have a drink.

At the end of the Prado, we were approached by a woman asking if we knew how she could get to the large Castillo on the other side of the bay. When I explained that she would have to take either a bus or a ferry to reach it, she asked where we were going, and if she could join us. When travelling solo, you have to have the nerve to ask people if you can accompany them – after all, the worst thing that can happen is that they say no.

My first hint that she was going to be trouble was when I asked her if she was travelling by herself and I received a lecture telling me that it isn't just men who can travel alone, but women can too. Well, OK then! I was only trying to make conversation.

While we strolled along, she told us she was from Germany, had been in Veradero, and was spending her last few days in Cuba in Havana. As we conversed, it seemed like everything she was telling us was her way of teaching us about Cuba. I just let her ramble on, not bothering to tell her that this was my twelfth visit. She told us that she had got Cuban pesos from the bank, and was using them, albeit with some trouble. I couldn't figure out how a tourist was able to obtain Cuban pesos, but Carene's opinion was that she had probably made such a fuss at the bank that they gave them to her just to get her out of their hair. The kicker was when, with a concerned look on her face, she asked me, like I was a feeble old woman, if I was okay walking. I assured her I was fine. When we talked about dancing salsa, she asked in amazement, "You dance salsa?" When she said that Cuban men aren't very good dancers, I couldn't even reply. Later, when I told Juan that bit of news, the look on his face was priceless. I had just about had my fill of our new friend, and we hadn't even arrived at the hotel yet.

Back at the Inglaterra, I put a bag of gifts together for the Lazaros and we met Juan in the lobby to walk the short distance for our visit.

When we arrived, we stopped at Gramma's apartment to say hello. She obviously knew we were coming and greeted us with big hugs and kisses. Lazaro came down to greet us and I found him to be quite emotional, which made me feel somewhat guilty that I hadn't made a point of visiting them on my last few trips. Upstairs, Mariela welcomed us, telling us that unfortunately we wouldn't be seeing Melina or Kmilo. They didn't know that we were visiting, and were gone for the day.

Lazaro told us that he was now working for the Historic Society, diving and taking pictures of underwater relics, and that Kmilo was also working with him. Juan told me later that because I had given Lazaro a camera a few years previously, I had opened the door for him.

Yonmay, the older brother who lives with Gramma, came up to see us, telling us that his son, now two years old, was doing well and living with his mother. Yonmay and the boy's mother were no longer together, but remain friendly.

We had café and a very nice visit while catching up on each other's news. I made a vow to myself that I would visit the family whenever I'm in Havana.

Since Juan was ready for our night out, he waited in the lobby while Carene and I went up and did a quick change. Our plan was dinner at La Terraza and then some bar-hopping. When I'm in Cuba, I like to treat Juan to a special dinner, and La Terraza was the perfect place for it. The restaurant, located on an upper floor in a large building, has a lovely outdoor dining area, and everything is cooked over an open flame. There is nothing nicer than a warm Cuban night, with a soft breeze, while indulging in fabulous food. When a trio came to the table and played two of my favourite Cuban songs, I was in heaven.

There is a bar in Old Havana called Sloppy Joes that was a popular spot for celebrities to frequent back in the day. After being closed for forty-eight years, it reopened in 2013, so I wanted to check it out. It is a large space and still has the original single-piece mahogany bar which is beautiful. It happened to be Hallowe'en night, so we were met with servers dressed in costume, giving me the feeling we were in for a fun night.

I was quite full from dinner so I ordered a Limoncello on ice. I had thought about ordering a double, but remembered in Cuba they free pour. I received what seemed like a triple, with a small bucket of ice on the side. Carene ordered sangria, which arrived over-sized and fancy. Juan loves brandy, so I ordered him a Remy Martin, and after taking his first sip, his eyes rolled back in his head with delight.

People began arriving in costumes that were quite elaborate, and the whole thing was making us laugh. When a group came in dressed as the Pope, a Cardinal and Satan, Juan, being a good Catholic, didn't seem to be very impressed.

I ordered another Limoncello, and again received a huge shot. After pouring, the waiter began to walk away, then realizing the bottle was almost empty, returned and emptied the remains into my glass.

On the way back to the hotel, as we walked across the park, I not only had a case of the giggles, but found that I could speak Español fluently, or so I thought.

Today, we would be visiting Muraleando. We wouldn't be seeing Manolo and Mayra as they were in Mexico City visiting their son Manoly. He had moved there to work as a photographer, but was now doing modelling. It seems when he was doing a shoot, someone thought he was so good-looking that they approached him about becoming a model. Apparently he is achieving much success in his new career.

Muraleando had recently won the very prestigious *Premio Nacional de Cultura Communitaria* award for 2014. When they called Manolo in Mexico to tell him the news, he cried with joy.

A lunch had been arranged for us at Manolo's, so at the appointed time we walked over. Mayra's sister-in-law and a lady from the neighbourhood had prepared the meal, and it was delicious. Mayra's mother, Erminda, was there to visit with us. She told us that she was missing Mayra terribly. Since they live one floor apart in the same house, I understood completely.

Juan and Jesús picked us up right on time and we reluctantly said good-bye to Havana. At the airport there were hugs and kisses all around, with promises to see them soon.

After breezing through check-in, we went upstairs to the departure lounge and did what has become my routine when I'm departing from

Varadero. We took a seat at the counter of the snack bar and ordered two sandwiches and two cafés.

Carene had come down with a terrible cold, and Juan had advised her to have a shot of rum. While she did what she was told, I ordered my last delicious Cuban café. Before long it was time to bid farewell to my beloved Cuba.

Bonnie Martin

More Observations and Reflections - 2014

Cuban people care a lot for animals. Be it a beloved pet, or a stray, they are all treated with kindness. When they see an animal in need, they don't just ignore it, but go out of their way to help the animal.

After touring many state-owned facilities, such as small museums, one has to wonder how they manage to keep such places open when most of the time there is no one going through them. My reasoning is that Cuba takes its history seriously, and appreciates what their forefathers did for the country. You always receive a warm welcome from the guides, I think partly because they love their work, and partly because they are happy to have someone to talk to.

In most countries, some people have complaints about the country in which they reside, and Cuba is no different. Yes, there are some that would like to leave, but many love their country and would never live anywhere else.

Like cities everywhere, some people live in undesirable conditions. Because people flock to the cities in search of jobs, there just isn't the space to house them all.

Section Nine

July 2015

The tomb of "The Miraculous One", Necrópolis Colón – 2015

Trinidad – 2015

Juan, Bonnie, Trinidad – 2015

Muraleando – 2015

School children, Las Terrazas – 2015

Tossing flowers for Camilo Cienfuegos, Las Terrazas – 2015

My Love Affair with Cuba

Bonnie, Cirilo, Barbara and grandson, Las Terrazas - 2015

Chapter Twenty-Six

The final trip I'll write about was a special one for me because my son, Derek, was finally able to accompany me. We would visit in July, and if we could survive the heat, would be there for the July 26 holiday, always an exciting time.

We exited the airport in Varadero to find Juan's smiling face to greet us. After hugs and introductions we were on our way, stopping in Mantanza for lunch, and arriving at the Hotel Inglaterra in the early evening. I invited Juan to join us later for a light dinner and some drinks. We went to Sloppy Joe's and all ordered Cuban sandwiches, which seemed appropriate, and then toasted being in Cuba.

For our first day in Havana, Juan and Jesús met us at the hotel and took us on a walking tour in Habana Vieja. On our walk we came upon a human statue – a man, made up with bronze makeup, standing very still. I had seen one the previous year, and it had taken me a while to figure it out. This particular one was made to look like Jesse James, and as we stood looking at him, he seemed to be staring at me in a mischievous way. Acting like an old pro, I told Derek to put some money in his bag, but when he did, the statue didn't move. As we took some pictures with Derek standing beside him, Jesse James kept staring at me with the same mischievous look, which was making me giggle nervously. When he still didn't move, I went and stood on his other side for a picture of the three of us. Just as we went to leave, Jesse grabbed me from behind, putting his gun to my head. I let out a scream so loud I'm sure they heard me for blocks. By now a crowd had gathered and everyone, including me was laughing. Jesse bid me adieu with a kiss on my hand.

Arrangements had been made for a visit to Muraleando so we freshened up at the hotel, gathered up some gifts and then headed there. A tour was just leaving when we arrived so many of the artists were there. I took Derek into El Tanque to view the art and then Victor gave him a tour around the site, pointing out the latest additions. We were asked to have a seat in the reception area, and with the artists watching, a musical presentation was put on for us. At the end of the performance, Victor made a very nice speech, thanking me for my contributions, saying I help make it possible for them to accomplish what they do. When I realized that everyone had stayed, and the performance was put on just for us, it touched me deeply.

Manolo and Mayra were in Mexico, so I wouldn't be seeing them. When there was no sign of Mayra's mother, Erminda, I inquired and was told that she had fallen recently, so was taking it easy. I asked her son Tony if I could visit her and he replied that she was hoping I would.

A Moment in Time - Derek does the patio

The Hotel Inglaterra is located in a busy area of Havana. A large patio at the front of the hotel is usually very busy, making it a happening spot, great for people watching. One of Derek's favourite things to do before we'd go out for the evening was to sit there with a beer while watching all of the action. When I joined him, he usually had stories to relay to me about his experiences. He was constantly approached by ladies of the evening, and once by a transvestite. What I found funny was that even after I joined him, the ladies still wouldn't leave him alone.

I was taking the Lazaro family out for dinner. Juan had prearranged everything, choosing a small restaurant in their neighbourhood to enable them to walk there. There were eleven of us, and we had a wonderful time. Juan certainly earned his money, constantly translating for us. We all had to laugh when he excused himself to go to the restroom, and we all just sat staring at each other.

I went and sat beside Kmilo and, with Juan translating, told him it was his turn to receive a special gift from me. He sat listening with a big smile on his face as I presented him with a card containing some money, telling him that I hoped it would help him with his plans for the future. I was rewarded with a lovely kiss.

Derek was enjoying himself immensely. Between the mojitos he was drinking, and the beers he had consumed at the Inglaterra in the afternoon, he was very caught up in the moment. We were nearly ready to leave when he announced he wanted to make a toast, so we all ordered another drink. He made a heart-felt speech, telling the family that he had heard so much about them through the years, and could now see why they mean so much to me. Of course, it brought me to tears.

Outside, we took some group photos, and after lots of hugs and kisses, said our good-byes until next time.

On this, our final day in Havana, our first stop was *Plaza de la Revolución* (Revolution Square). I had been past the site numerous times, but never up close, always thinking it to be a huge concrete obelisk, sitting in the middle of a large open field, and quite ugly.

*Plaza de la Revolución is Cuba's political, administrative and cultural centre. What had been known as the Plaza Civica was renamed Plaza de la Revolución following Fidel Castro's victory in 1959 and the government was moved there. Government buildings surround the square, and on the façade of two buildings are huge bronze wire sculptures of two of Cuba's military heroes, Che Guevara and Camilo Cienfuegos.
In the middle of the plaza is the Memorial José Martí. It consists of a 109 m tower and a fifty-nine-foot white marble statue of José Martí. The actual memorial is in the interior of the base.

I noticed some different buses in Havana and asked Jesús about them. He explained that there was now a new bus co-op operating in

Havana, a spin on socialism that is working very well. The state supplies the buses, and all of the employees are members of the co-op. They have found that because there is no bureaucracy, the people take great pride in their job and problems such as theft are nearly non-existent.

Chapter Twenty-Seven

We left Havana, travelling to Trinidad, where we stayed for two nights. Our casa, in the older section of town was charming, with a lovely patio on the roof where we could relax, and where we would take our breakfast.

Out exploring, we came across some music, always something that I love. On a wide set of stone steps that led to a church, a unique area had been set up. A stage on one side of the stairs had a full band playing. There were tables and chairs that allowed people to sit with a drink while listening to music. Juan said that at night the stairs were always packed with people.

Through the years, I have tried to learn as much as I could about Cuban history, but I had never thought much about the time right after the Revolution, and how the struggle continued. Going through a small museum in Trinidad that focused on the Revolution, Juan relayed stories about some of the atrocities that took place which put that time into perspective for me.

When Fidel began a literacy campaign in 1961, he sent teachers, some as young as ten years, into the hills and countryside to teach the peasants how to read and write. There were some who were trying to undo what the revolutionaries had fought to achieve. These mercenaries would make raids on homes, killing and torturing the teachers, not caring how young they were.

It's funny how you can visit a place, and on a subsequent visit, see it in a different light. Staying in a casa in the old section of town and visiting different places did that for me in Trinidad. We had spent two afternoons listening to fantastic music, eaten delicious meals, and spent two relaxing evenings on our patio, with Derek and Juan enjoying cigars. At one point, Derek stated to me, "I could sit and talk with Juan forever."

We left Trinidad, arriving in Cienfuegos close to midday. It was just too hot to do much, so after walking downtown for lunch, we headed back to our casa, turned on the air conditioning, and had siestas. I knew Cuba was going to be hot when we decided to visit in July, but nothing could prepare us for this kind of heat and humidity.

On our last day in Cuba, we toured all around the town square, checking out many of the buildings while learning more about Cuban history. In one of the older buildings we came upon a boy and girl, about ten years of age, having a dance lesson. They were being taught by two teachers, a man and a woman and, after watching for a while, I realized just how dedicated the students, as well as the teachers were. The young couple danced for a short time, and then as the boy sat quietly waiting, one of the teachers worked with the girl to perfect a move. It was done over and over until they got it just right. In a waiting area for parents, a sign read: NO PARENTS PERMITTED IN THE DANCE STUDIO. There would be no stage parents here.

An old castle in the Punta Gorda area, Palacio de Valle, built by a wealthy sugar merchant in 1917, and turned into a casino by Batista, is now an upscale restaurant. The castle has a terrace bar on the roof, where, for a nominal fee which includes a cocktail, you can relax with a drink while taking in the view. Beside the castle is the Hotel Jagua which was built by Batista's brother in the 1950s. We looked around and after checking out the prices, which were quite reasonable, thought it seemed like a nice place to stay on a future visit.

I love exploring off the beaten track, so I suggested that we go for a drive along the bus route that Juan and I had travelled on in 2011. We passed through small villages and resort areas ending up very close to a Castillo we had visited then.

After dinner, we went to the upper level of the casa, where the sky was bright with a rare blue moon. A light breeze was welcome after the intense heat of the past few days. Derek and Juan were enjoying their last cigars together and sipping rum, while I drank mojitos. As we sat just enjoying one another's company, there it was yet again, that mushy feeling in my stomach. It was a perfect end to a fantastic holiday.

Epilogue - The sum of it all

This profound change in my life began ten short years ago, and changed the person I am today. I believe it was all meant to be, or as I have said many times, it was the angels at work.

After fourteen trips to Cuba, I've managed to discover a large part of the island, seen beauty that took my breath away, and witnessed a completely different way of life. I've made many friends there and, as my circle of friends grew, I became acquainted with some of the most interesting people one could hope to know.

My visits have had many highlights, but I think the biggest was being presented with "The Key to Muraleando" in 2009, making me a bona fide member of the community. I am now referred to as a "Godmother of Muraleando", which is a great honour.

Another highlight of my Cuban experience was discovering Las Terrazas, one of the most beautiful places I have ever been. I like to think of Las Terrazas as my own personal Utopia.

Many changes have taken place in Cuba since I first visited, and numerous predictions made as to what will take place there in the future. I'm sure that whatever occurs, the people of Cuba will handle it the way they handle most occurrences in their lives, with dignity and a huge smile.

I had to conclude this book at some point, but that doesn't mean my visits will cease. As long as I'm able, I plan on returning to Cuba, a place I have grown to love.

Sources

Eyewitness Travel Guides – Cuba

Amelia Goyri de la Hoz
Barrio Chino
Casa de Don Tomás
Casa Particulares
Castillo del Morro
Centro Habana and Prado
Cienfuegos
Cojímar
Cristo de la Habana
Ernest Hemingway
Estacion Ecologia
Habana Vieja
Manaca Iznaga Estate
Miramar
Mogotes
Mural de la Prehistoria
Necrópolis Colón
Parque Lenin
Plaza de la Revolución
Rumba
Sancti Spíritus
Santería
Soroa
The Malecón
Valley de los Ingenios
Vedado and Plaza
Viñales

Wikipedia

    CDRs
    José Fuster

www.cuba-junky.com

    Polo Montanez

Printed in the United States
By Bookmasters